Building a Strong Safety Culture
The 5 C's of Workplace Safety

"Safety First and Always" is one of the core values at Satellite Shelters. As the VP of Human Resources, one of my challenges is to always make sure to keep that value on the forefront of every employee's mind. This book, describing the 5 C's, not only provides a framework to make sure our safety culture is maintained, it also supports that framework with relevant stories. As a long time client of OECS, I can say that they have hit the nail on the head again with a captivating read; which is not easy to do in the safety world! — Michele Pipitone, VP, Human Resources, Satellite Shelters, Inc.

Far too many companies and leaders struggle to implement the best tools and practices for daily workplace safety consistently. In this book, Tim and Chris share their expertise, real life examples and stories that make it much quicker and easier to understand and apply. This book is an excellent guide to creating a safety mindset and integrating that into your culture along with the 5 C's. This book is a must-read whether you are an owner, manager or work in the shop or field. Well done OECS. – John P. Palen, Founder & CEO, Allied Executives

Building a Strong Safety Culture
The 5 C's of Workplace Safety

By Tim Sheehan, Chris Naylor and the OSHA + Environmental Compliance Systems Team (OECS)

For information, please contact:

OECS, OSHA/Environmental Compliance Systems
1000 Shelard Parkway, #140
Saint Louis Park, MN 55426

Phone 763-417-9599
info@oecscomply.com

This book is dedicated to our OECS Associates and hundreds of clients who are committed to building strong safety cultures day in and day out.

It is published in memory of the thousands who have lost their lives in workplace accidents who inspire leaders to step up and commit to safety across the world.

We are thankful for the guidance and support from Jim Wilson at PathForeWord® who helped make this book possible.

Table of Contents

Introduction

To get started, Tim Sheehan shares a pivotal moment in his safety journey. This moment launched a lifetime mission to bring safety to organizations to allow their workers to get home safely from work every day.

Big Joe

At the early stages of my career in retail, I would hear about the "Big Joe" story from time to time. However, it was in bits and pieces, never fully explained or understood. It had happened a few years earlier. One day I was able to corner one of the operations leaders for the company I worked for at the time and asked, "What happened?"

He paused, looked at me and then stared out the window of my store in Minnetonka, Minnesota. He went on to say the company had just recently opened stores in Texas, a far stretch for a small company based in the Midwest.

At one of the stores, a couple with their toddler son was shopping in the TV department positioned in the far back of the store. They asked one of the Blue Shirts in the department for help with finding a new TV. While they were shopping, the toddler had wandered off into another aisle of TVs, out of the sight of his parents, for just a moment.

In the aisle next to his parents, another Blue Shirt was operating a Big Joe forklift. This piece of equipment was standard for many retailers to move inventory either up or down from the racking above the aisles. In this case, the employee had gotten on the platform, hit the switch to ride straight up and reached the top of the racking.

Once they were at the top of the racking, they loaded a heavy TV onto the platform and hit the switch to lower themselves back to the store floor.

In the split moment, the toddler had crawled underneath the Big Joe platform and was crushed instantly. The parents came running around the corner to find their son dead. This all happened in literally seconds.

The leader who told me this story got emotional. His voice was quiet, and his eyes fixed on mine. This was entirely out of character for him. His voice was usually measured in decibels and could be heard through thick walls! He said, "Tim, this tragedy haunts me to this day. I feel for the parents and the loss of their son. Every time something like this happens in your life, it causes you to reflect on what could have been done to avoid it altogether. I've replayed the story a thousand times. It all could have been avoided."

He went on to say, "It's this event that has motivated a handful of us to see to it this never happens again."

I instantly understood why he was so passionate about my store and all the others, taking safety training seriously. That's what prompted me to ask the question. You see, I didn't want to have my team take the training. At first, I was resistant and thought it was a waste of time. But now, the story was a wake-up call.

That experience brings to the forefront several valuable lessons, The kind that can help tackle safety at your company. The power of storytelling is one of these lessons. Sharing his story and how it came from the heart directly impacted me.

The 5 C's of Safety in Action

You can see from this story that it takes a real **commitment** to safety as the starting point for any organization.

Then there are the ongoing efforts to get in **compliance** with safety procedures, practices and training. As was the case with the retailer's story earlier, they knew, sadly, the true impact of doing less than the best.

The "Big Joe" story also said a lot about the company's **culture** at the time. One of the core values was to "learn from challenge and change." This was now the mantra that a small company used to take full responsibility for becoming a big one.

Unfolding things even further, you can see that, in this case, the operations leader was a true safety **champion**. He said, "We are going to make sure this doesn't happen again."

Ultimately, the **cost** of the tragedy in human life and to the brand name of a young company was staggering. Grasping the magnitude of this impact is what drives so many leaders and safety professionals today.

If you're tracking along, yes – that's the 5 C's in action!

OECS Yesterday and Today

Founded in 1993, through its safety associates' hard work and dedication, OSHA Environmental Compliance Systems (OECS) grew over 30 years to become a leading workplace safety consulting company – with offices in the Twin Cities and Fargo.

Then in 2017, Tim Sheehan and his wife, Chris Naylor, were fortunate enough to have the opportunity to become the proud owners of OECS. Their goal was to expand its safety reach, offering additional safety services and a world-class customer experience for their safety clients. And, just as important, the new owners were passionate about creating a top place to work for their growing number of safety associates.

Fueled by their passion for safety and a strong desire to make a difference in the lives of workers and their companies, today, OECS helps create safe work environments for thousands of employees throughout the Midwest, pushing their clients to go beyond compliance to develop strong safety cultures.

That's where the 5 C's were born! Together with the passionate and highly experienced team of OECS safety professionals, this simple framework was formulated – and it has been used successfully to help their clients, both in manufacturing and construction, discover a way to think about, engage with and improve safety at their company!

The company mission of OECS is *to inspire strong safety cultures that keep employees returning home safe*. They, along with their entire team, feel strongly that **The 5 C's of Safety** can help you accomplish the same mission!

Chapter 1 — THE 5 C's of Safety and You

"The economic waste resulting from carelessness is appalling, but anyone who stops for a moment to consider the sorrow and desolation which is brought into thousands of lives each year by utter thoughtlessness must feel a new resolve to make a habit of "Safety First."

— W. C. Durant, President, General Motors 1920

Got Milk?

It appears to be a simple business, making milk. But this business is anything but when it comes to safety.

Their best-ever no-lost-days stood at 1,633. That's over four years. Four years and almost 25 more weeks to boot.

How do they do this? What made it possible for these folks in this nondescript building to do what so many other companies only dream about?

Enter their supervisor, Don. He's been on point for safety during most of his career. He follows the plan. He's got the compliance part of this down.

Also, enter Ari Cook, the OECS associate who works with Don and his company; they were in sync the moment Ari entered the facility.

Ari engaged with Don and his team, observing what was going on and preparing to deliver that month's training topic – Heat Stress. That's a well-timed topic during May in South Dakota when it starts getting hot.

Ari's training session was impressive with its interactive approach and personalized stories on the topic. Ari's energy and enthusiasm for the topic was top-notch.

Even more impressive was that Don quietly made sure every employee in the plant attended one of the training sessions. Don wasn't going to let anyone miss out on the OECS monthly on-site training, one of the hallmarks of an excellent safety strategy.

A Leader's Commitment

Don knew who was supposed to be at each of the three sessions – one at 7 pm, 8:30 pm and 10 pm. He worked the facility to find the stragglers and get them in their seats. He knew who the new workers were in the plant and that they were likely unsure where and what to do when it came to "safety training." It was like watching a scoutmaster collect his troops scattered throughout the woods to gather them around the campfire.

Ari was in rare form, spinning safety tales about a golf outing that went bad, a co-worker who fainted while driving a forklift, and the time heat stress took the life of Minnesota Viking's Korey Stringer. All these examples happened because people put themselves at unnecessary risk and didn't watch for warning signs.

Don had heard a version of all this many times before. But he wanted to make sure every single person on his team heard it, too. For many of them, this was their first time. They took it in, asked Ari some questions and the 30-minute training flew by.

When Don was asked afterward, "How did you guys create a four-year plus window of zero lost days? And now you're off starting another string. What are some of your secrets?"

He didn't take long to respond. "We follow the plan OECS outlined for us. We take the training component seriously. We track who attends. If they miss, we have make-up sessions. We ensure they have the information they need to do their job safely. It's not complicated."

It seemed too easy. Not only that, but training is just one component of many that go into a strong safety culture. Don embodied every one of the 5 C's.

His **commitment** was evident. The first C. His engagement in the safety process, including his participation in the training, was a very visual demonstration to his team about his commitment.

He was all over their **compliance**, the second C, with training, written programs, attention to safety audits and so on. He had established a strong foundation.

From this foundation, the company worked to strengthen their safety **culture**, the third C, by establishing the internal record they did for no lost days, celebrating the milestones along the way – T-shirts, pizza parties, etc. It was embedded as part of their DNA.

The fourth C, **champions**, was no more visible than Don himself. When people see the top tier of leadership supports safety, people like Don step up and take the mantle. That's precisely what Don has been doing. He is one of their safety champions, for sure.

Costs, the fifth C, helps keep all this effort in focus. The bottom-line savings from better workers comp insurance premiums and fewer production interruptions due to injuries are to name only two. Don's plant has enjoyed these savings and more over the years.

But they also reaped the reward of the ultimate "cost avoidance" – saving people's lives. The "cost" of losing a loved one, co-worker and friend is the ultimate cost we all want to avoid!

As you can tell, it is often the "unsung" heroes like both Don and Ari who are going about doing their jobs every day. They make all the difference in the world of safety.

That's why it's important to share more stories like Don's and more insight into how the 5 C's can help steer your company to new heights in safety!

Keeping it Simple

When you boil it down to learning new things, OECS has always been big believers in "simplicity over complexity." With that said, workplace safety is a complex topic. It spans volumes of regulations, dives deep into the sciences and becomes a life-or-death matter for millions.

But this is the challenge: There is a whole bunch of stuff millions of workers need to know but not enough time to address, along with a general lack of safety leadership.

As Mark Shields, a Lead Safety Associate with OECS, recently noted when visiting a client's manufacturing facility, "These guys are busy. They don't have time to research answers about safety regulations or create training materials and so on. We have to simplify safety for them." So true. OECS clients are running plants, pressing out parts, building condos and everything else in between.

The 5 C's Explained

You can see that building a strong safety culture doesn't happen unless there is a **commitment** from leadership first. This is where the safety movement must start – leadership.

Chapter 1 — THE 5 C's of Safety and You

If you're waiting for the owner or another key leader to light the fire, you might be disappointed. That's why they have you! You're the fire; you picked this book up or were given it for a reason.

Once leadership is committed, the team can roll up their sleeves and begin to understand what's at the foundation of a strong safety culture: A team focused on being in safety **compliance** for their company, in their industry and for the benefit of their people.

From there, the groundwork is laid for building a strong safety **culture**. The team needs to see committed members of leadership who grasp safety fundamentals and actively support getting into safety compliance. Now leveraging the good parts of the company's DNA or culture can be channeled into building an even stronger safety culture.

Along the journey, people within the company will sense real support or "air cover" from leadership when it comes to safety. What happens in this process is magic – **champions** from all levels within the organization begin to emerge. They step up and step into the movement. Simply said, champions are less about quantity and more about quality. They are the game-changers.

An exciting outcome of this effort is something that can be a difference-maker in your highly competitive industry. Your **cost**s, as measured in many ways, can go down. The business case for safety will expose you to the many ways your safety journey can improve your company's bottom line. More critical, investing the time here can help you avoid the ultimate cost – of losing a human life.

But notice safety doesn't start there. Instead, the financial impact is an outcome of what began with leadership commitment, focused on compliance and leveraging safety as a catalyst for strengthening the **overall** company culture, not just safety.

"You are Now in Charge of Safety."

Have you ever heard this before? Or "Hey, the boss just said we're no good at safety and need to start paying more attention." Or even worse, "We're in trouble after that last accident; OSHA is coming to investigate!"

YOU are not alone. OECS has worked with hundreds of small to mid-sized manufacturing and construction firms facing the same dilemma. Most want to do better in safety. Most are stretched too thin. And most eventually find a SPARK, someone or some series of events become the catalyst to drive the safety culture to the next level!

Tim Peterson, CHST, OECS VP of Operations and Sales, says, "It's not uncommon for the least interested or prepared person on the leadership team to be handed the safety responsibility. But these are often great people who care about the company and its team. With the right support and commitment, they can go on to become great safety leaders!"

These scenarios and many more have become the catalyst for leaders to decide to do something about safety at their company. Maybe something like this got you to pick up this book. Or perhaps your company is making a serious commitment to safety, and you want to find a way to bring it to the next level.

It's in Your Hands

As a leader, whatever the scenario is, you've just put a powerful tool in your hands to help achieve your safety goals! OECS has been in the safety business for 30 years. The highly experienced team of safety consultants has seen a lot. They want to share this with you in a way that can have an immediate positive impact. Most importantly, they want to help bring your team home safe every day.

This safety experience or said another way — perspective — is what makes this book unique. The team has had extensive military experience across the globe, decades with Minnesota and Federal OSHA, and years in both construction and general industry. Not just in safety but doing the jobs that include real work. For example, construction laborers, manufacturing workers and so many more.

Consider this: By reading this book and applying some of the lessons they've learned, you can put your company in a much better position to accomplish your safety goals! And most important, inspire a strong safety culture that keeps your employees returning home safe!

Chapter 2 — Safety Mindset and the Power of Storytelling

"I've personally met up with quite a few legless, armless and other badly messed-up folks. There's a whole lot of mighty serious accident contemplation going on in our hospitals. My observations have taught me that it is much better to think about accidents before they happen than to brood on them afterward. Personally, I'd rather be late for dinner tonight here than to be on time for breakfast in the next world in the morning. Haste makes waste of a lot of good human material."
— Irvin S. Cobb, author, humorist, and editor 1876 - 1944

Before we dive further into the 5C's of safety, it's essential to consider two critical elements of your safety journey. First, you must develop, embrace and exude a safety mindset when approaching this work. Second, safety doesn't need to be boring or put people on the defensive. It's life-changing work, in a good way. Storytelling is one of the greatest tools you can deploy to transmit the lessons and motivations to those you're trying to influence!

Why You, Why Now?

"Why You?" Somebody gave you this book. Or maybe you even bought it, which is better still. Regardless of how you got here, things do happen for a reason. It's essentially, "Tag; you're it!" YOU are the one who can make the difference. Or else your boss, the owner, your safety partner, whoever, would not have bothered to give you a copy.

Change rarely happens in one big sweeping event. Instead, it often comes one step at a time, in small batches, building on top of one initiative after another.

To back that up, Gartner reports that, on average, organizations have gone through five significant firmwide changes in the past three years. On top of that, nearly 75% expect that rate of change to increase over the next three years.[1]

Change is the only constant in our world. But fortunately, organizations realize that lasting change only comes from engaged employees.

That means they have recognized YOU as one of the significant pieces of the "safety puzzle" that leadership in your company is trying to solve. That's the simple answer to – "Why You?"

"Why Now?" Good question. If meaningful, substantive change comes in steps, then the sheer act of you picking up this book and beginning to apply it is a start. In fact, it's a big deal.

It's a big deal because your leadership team and your employees will notice when YOU start to internalize and apply the safety lessons in this book.

It's a bit like the "butterfly effect" in chaos theory. Small things can have an enormous ripple effect in a complex system. At its most simplistic, the concept suggests that the flapping of a butterfly's wings could eventually cause a typhoon. In other words, small changes can lead to large-scale effects over time!

---

[1] Reference https://www.gartner.com/en/human-resources/insights/organizational-change-management

The Right Mindset or "Distilling the Truth"

Tim Peterson, CHST, OECS VP of Operations and Sales, had been working with a client who ran a distillery for years. His key contact there is a perfect example of having the right mindset.

Somewhere along the line, she was leading the charge for safety at her facility, not only by title but by sheer passion and will. Tim had been working with her for years.

It was clear she had the right mindset in her approach. She was open to new ideas, patient with a department and their safety concerns while at the same time getting right after another group that was lagging in training. She had her hands firmly on her company's safety steering wheel.

Somewhere along the line, she got tagged. She was it. When asked, "How did you become the safety 'lightning rod' at your company?" She paused for a minute and said, "Somebody had to get the job done!" Then stormed off down the production line, making sure a batch of liquor was getting packaged correctly and safely.

Tim Peterson later said about her, "Some time ago, she picked up the safety baton and hasn't looked back since. She is the glue. She keeps it all together and helps everyone head down the track in the right direction. She has a strong grasp of the safety fundamentals and keeps pushing to go to the next level."

Don't Let Perfect Be the Enemy of Good.

It was 100+ degrees with even a higher "feels like" temperature. The client's plant director told our safety associate, Natalie Blackwell, she had limited time to complete the training. The reason being, with temperatures so high, power consumption was peaking, and they were participating in an energy-saving program.

With the chips down, she quickly set up the safety training session while the leadership team ushered in the thirty or so workers to hear Natalie's topic. It was a race against the clock before things shut down. All the while, with the shop floor garage doors wide open for a bit of airflow, all that came in was a hot breeze. Not your typical Minnesota summer day.

At first, one might feel for the participants and Natalie, acknowledging this was less than ideal for everyone involved! Why not just reschedule and send everybody home early? Wait for next month.

Instead, Natalie and the leadership team quickly conferred beforehand and agreed they needed to press forward. They felt skipping the training, even in less-than-ideal circumstances, would send the wrong message. Staying on course to their regular training plan implied they were genuinely committed to safety, come thick or thin.

They believed it would be better to provide the training and have at least some seep in with their team versus delaying any longer. Plus, they didn't want to risk potential injuries because their team had a training gap related to the topic at hand.

The truth is that your approach to safety will have an enormous impact on many people. Approaching this awesome duty with the right mindset is an important start.

Why Stories Matter or Man Down!

Danny Hoffman, a safety associate with OECS, spent 30 years in the U.S. Army. Yes, he has some stories to tell! He recently conducted safety training on heat stress at an OECS client facility. Overall, the training was going fine, and the small group of about 20 installers was paying attention.

Then Danny started to tell a story. He explained how he was with a soldier in training at Fort Ripley in northern Minnesota. The soldier was lying on the ground unconscious. Heatstroke. He didn't correctly follow the advice to manage his body's heat in the hot July Minnesota sun. He was in danger, requiring a medical helicopter to land on the training field and rush him to a local hospital. "We didn't know if he was going to make it," Danny said in a quiet voice.

Danny shared more details about how the soldier eventually made it through days later. He switched gears and went on to draw parallels to situations the audience could personally relate to – like grandparents out in the hot sun watching their grandkids play sports. Or kids out running up and down a field without water breaks. Then there is the ongoing challenge of staying hydrated when consuming the wrong type of liquid could be deadly.

The story was an excellent choice for the topic. It had a significant impact because it came from someone personally involved. Power also came from Danny's body language as he unpacked the story. The entire group leaned in, got quiet in the room and hung on every word. This is a superb example of the power of storytelling.

Stories serve as a potent vehicle for communicating a company's vision, mission, values and the journey necessary to accomplish your goals.

In the book *Unleash the Power of Storytelling,* Rob Biesenbach does an excellent job of laying out a roadmap on how to do this. Rob explains why it's so important that leaders raise their business storytelling skills to the next level. In fact, from a safety perspective, because of the seriousness of the topic to people's lives, storytelling is one of the most critical skills a leader must possess.

Another helpful resource is the book, *Speak like Churchill, Stand Like Lincoln*, by James C. Humes. With two visionary leaders like Churchill and Lincoln, you can imagine that there must be story advice embedded in the "21 Powerful Secrets of History's Greatest Speakers," as the book says.

Sure enough, there is. The punchline from the author is this: When it comes to telling stories, sharing from your own experience is often the most powerful. We often underestimate our own life experiences and miss the opportunity to share a story that comes from the heart. Your audience can tell the difference.

The combination of these two points is vital to make upfront in this book. First, it's critical to choose the right mindset for taking on the safety challenge. Second, to build a strong safety culture, you must leverage the power of storytelling to communicate critical safety lessons that challenge attitudes and behaviors.

Last, visit the OECS website at **oecscomply.com** for video examples of how storytelling can convey critical safety learning points for your team.

Chapter 3 — Commitment: Starts at the Top

"Safety work is today recognized as an economic necessity. It is the study of the right way to do things."
- — Robert W. Campbell, first president of the National Safety Council, 1913

At the leadership level, the first C of the 5 C's, the **Commitment** to safety, is the linchpin of the entire five-step process we've outlined. Without commitment, nothing else works for very long.

Who is the Assassin?

One Sunday morning, when attending church, Pastor Joel K. Johnson of Westwood Community Church, in Chanhassen, Minnesota, got up to deliver his sermon. Pastor Joel has been in the business of saving souls for over 30 years. He gets your attention early! This sermon did just that. He said, "Procrastination in the assassination of motivation."

Tim Sheehan, OECS owner, hearing this, gave it some thought and couldn't listen to anything else. He wrote it down on the note page provided at the beginning of the service.

His mind started to process so many things – not only about the long road ahead for his own spiritual journey, but something also very important to him – writing this book!

Pastor Joel hits the mark on this one. Procrastination, which often tangles up leaders like a vine, prevents them from addressing vital issues like safety. This procrastination, then, literally "assassinates" the motivation to take action.

If you're a pastor saving souls or a business leader working on the safety of your employees, the heart of the matter is **commitment.**

Sometimes it takes a spark to get things going. And that spark for your company could be the *catalyst* right in front of you. What are you waiting for! (Yes, another C for added emphasis!)

The Catalyst for Change – What's Yours?

What's your company's catalyst for change? Is it a leadership team that thinks you're good but wants to be great? Maybe you've been tagged as the new "safety leader" and want to make a good impression on the leadership team about what you can do differently than before.

Or perhaps something even more dramatic has happened. A severe injury or fatality (SIF) has captured your company's attention. Maybe it's a change in leadership because the prior leader or team had more challenges with the business than they could handle. For example, it could be a new owner, CEO, or entire leadership team.

Whatever the reason or issues, embrace them! These experiences, or inflection points, are windows of time that create space for leaders to do amazing things!

Often leaders squander these opportunities. They duck, hide from the distress and some even run. They find another job. Or they wait until somebody comes and tells them to leave.

Instead of sticking your head in the sand, take on the mantle of safety leadership or make a substantial contribution as part of a team that leads for positive change in safety. Use the underlying series of events that led up to the point where you picked up this book as fuel for what may be a long but satisfying journey.

Regardless of how challenging, disappointing or frustrating, these events can ultimately push you through to the new challenges and opportunities you'll face in bringing safety to the next level at your company.

First Safety Book — A Learning Journey Begins

As noted in the last chapter, committed leadership is humble, always seeking help and advice and input from their team or anyone else with expertise for that matter.

One of the owners of OECS, Tim Sheehan, was determined to learn as much as he could after entering the safety business. One of the first books he read was, *7 Insights into Safety Leadership*, by Thomas R. Krause and Kristen J. Bell.

The authors said: "We discovered that the primary differentiating factor was the strength of safety leadership. Every other study in the series replicated and supported the central role of leadership in the success of safety improvement initiatives.

Unfortunately, relatively few senior leaders really, genuinely get safety. Far too few have personally invested themselves in safety."

The OECS team has found that unless a person has learned from direct personal experience with life-threatening, life-altering or life-ending events, they are unlikely to take on safety as their personal calling.

The critical point here is the lack of general understanding: *"Even among executives who have a strong motivation to lead safety…many do not understand what they need to do to achieve their goals."*

Here's the simple reason, when you think of the 5 C's of Safety, that a commitment by leadership is at the heart and soul of it all.

It's as Simple as GREAT versus BAD Leadership

When you begin to distill the learnings from stories in this book and from your own experience, you begin to recognize some interesting comparisons. Look at this outline and visualize what a great safety leader looks like versus a bad one.

About Safety	Great Safety Leadership	Bad Safety Leadership
Commitment	It's real, you can see it	Lip service at best
What they SAY	Talk about safety	Not much
What they DO	Actions match their words	Inconsistent with safe practices
Have a plan	In writing and understood	Maybe under that "pile over there"
Train employees	On a regular basis	No time to train
Audit for safety	Inspect what you expect	Too busy putting out fires
Accountability	Hold people accountable	Unsafe practices allowed to slide
Input from team	Ask for and value it	Avoid it, already know it all
Get Help + Advice	From wherever they can	Don't need it, we got it
Business Case	Understand the facts in lives and dollars	Clueless

When in the field, we've witnessed hundreds of companies in action day in and day out. This includes many leaders, both great and bad.

Great Leaders: Let's Dig In

First and foremost, **great safety leaders** really are committed to safety. They can't fake it. Employees can spot a faker a mile away. Instead, a good safety leader has their heart in it. They know what's at stake. This is an issue not only for themselves and their company but also for their co-workers and their own families as well. They are all in. Commitment is not in question.

Great leaders understand that over one million workers get injured in any given year, missing at least a day of work, and 5,000 die. They also believe most of this is avoidable!

Great safety leaders engage. They try to understand what is required to be in compliance. They do their homework and realize what's at stake if they do not have a basic working knowledge of the OSHA regulations applicable to their company and their business model.

They make sure there is a written plan in place that is understood by all and customized to their business. There is also real accountability for everyone involved.

They make sure their team gets trained on the plan. They work to ensure there is high-quality, regular ongoing training available for employees at every level of the organization. They take the time to participate in the training, making sure key issues are addressed and asking clarifying questions during the sessions to ensure everyone is clear on what they need to do.

Not only do they make sure their team is properly trained, but they check to make sure the training impacts where the rubber meets the road! They follow up and inspect what is taking place when it comes to safety. They perform visual checks constantly, ask questions routinely and dig in from time to time to make sure the core processes are tight.

They also ask for help. A genuine commitment to safety and every other aspect of the business includes being a humble leader, driven to learn. If they aren't already, they become a lifelong learner because LIVES are at stake. They lean on their team, peers, professional network, outside consultants, insurance company resources and even OSHA for advice, guidance and direction.

Great leaders clearly understand that the stakes are high – in both lives and dollars!

Great Leaders Build It from the Ground Up

Chad Preese was a new safety associate to OECS and, by all accounts, came through a different door than the other associates. Not general industry or construction, as is usually the case, but instead the hospitality industry.

While working at a large local hotel that was part of a global chain, his role evolved into taking on security and safety. For context, this hotel is huge and right in the center of downtown Minneapolis. It has played host to Super Bowls, conventions and other events, with guests from all over the world. The hotel eventually had to deal with massive civil unrest as well.

While the hotel was part of a large global chain, Chad was surprised to find no "playbook" for safety. "I had to figure it out on my own. Do the research, ask a lot of questions, roll-up my sleeves and apply what I was learning to my team's reality. "

"Initially, we lacked any focus, formal training, or accountability on safety. That's why it became part of my job. We worked hard to develop training that addressed some real challenges in housekeeping with language barriers. The same for maintenance where we had to address complex issues involved with operating a sprawling facility in the heart of a downtown area."

Chad went on to reflect on his experience, talking about how he got leadership engaged, built a safety plan piece-by-piece and held his team accountable for participating in training and getting actively involved in giving input on how to make their hotel safer.

What separated Chad from many other leaders charged with safety is this: He met and took on the challenge. He demonstrated many of the qualities of a great safety leader. And as a result, he earned himself a career at OECS.

Great Leaders Lead by Example

Working with hundreds of clients across the country, it's always exciting to hear about other excellent safety leadership. Mike Mockbee, who works with OECS clients in the southeastern part of the country, loves to go to Georgia. He loves to go to Georgia because one of his clients is a "safety rock star," as he calls them.

"When I visit for safety training and audits, they are ready. You can tell they are not faking it. The facility's housekeeping is second to none, the staff is bought into the safety plan, and they can't wait until I get there."

What? Can't wait until you get there? This is not your typical response to a safety consultant's visit. He elaborates. "They can't wait to show me how they've addressed and corrected all the issues from the last safety audit. There were not many issues, but it's how they attack it. They also want to share other improvements they are making to move to the next level in safety."

"Another thing that sets them apart from the rest is their leader will walk alongside me when I visit. He and his team will make adjustments or fix any safety-related issues literally in real-time! It's so crystal clear that this location stands out because they have a great safety leader. When compared to their peer locations across the company in other states, they are a standout!"

Bad Leaders: Let's Elaborate

Bad safety leaders are too busy. They don't have time to engage. Because business is so good or bad, it doesn't matter which one; there is a tremendous amount of firefighting going on. Therefore, it's a built-in excuse that doesn't allow them the time to engage in safety.

They do not understand, see the value in, or have the time to have a quality written plan in place. It's pretty much fly-by-the-seat-of-your-pants when it comes to safety.

Safety training? Oh my, get real. They can't fathom taking their team out of production or off the job site to get the proper training. This will COST the company valuable time and money. They feel safety is common sense anyhow, and if someone doesn't understand this, they probably shouldn't be working at this company.

Bad Leaders are the "No Shows"

Tim O'Connor, OHST, a Regional Safety Director at OECS, was at one of his clients preparing to give them their monthly safety training. This client ran a manufacturing facility with about 60 employees who would gather in two shifts to attend Tim's 30-minute safety training topic each month.

Tim noted before the training, "It's really telling. I've held many training events for this company, and not once has leadership shown up to participate. I tell leadership how important it is to lead by example and demonstrate their commitment to safety by showing up, but they won't listen. Regardless, we're making progress with them. But it could be so much more powerful if they would commit to getting more actively involved in the process!"

Tim spent 25 years serving and leading in the U.S. Army. He's seen the difference committed leadership makes. Frankly, there is no room for anything less especially when you imagine the kinds of situations they faced while deployed across the world to defend democracy.

Bad Leaders Create Risk

Bad leaders often have the attitude that there is no time for visually inspecting and coaching the team to ensure the right core processes are being followed. This includes safety. There are too many fires, they are too far behind, and the idea of walking around trying to add value in this way seems like a waste of time.

As far as getting help, that's not necessary. They've likely done the job for maybe five or 10+ years this way and made it this far. Why change now? And why would they want to ask for help within the company – which they feel is only a sign of weakness. Further still, getting help from the outside is not how their company operates. They believe in keeping to themselves, and if they don't go talking about their business with other people, they'll be fine.

Bad leaders don't understand that providing safety training can significantly reduce the likelihood of injuries and reduce related costs by as much as 40%. More on this later in the chapter on the business case for safety.

Andy Smoka, SMS, STSC and OECS safety associate, spent almost 30 years with Minnesota OSHA and has pretty much "seen it all." Andy has a fantastic life story that creates quite a backdrop to an equally fantastic safety career.

But first, to the training. OECS holds a monthly internal webinar focused on one topic an associate teaches the rest of the company. Andy chose fall protection because he had been getting a lot of questions from the team over the past several months.

For starters, the reason fall protection is so important is because in 2019 alone, 880 workers died, and 244,000 were injured badly enough to require days off work. In the construction industry, workers are at risk for falls more than seven times the rate of other industries. Fall protection is also the leading OSHA workplace safety citation.

Andy came prepared for his presentation. He had organized 89 slides with a different picture on every slide! This was a 60-minute session. That's right. He had 89 slides for a 60 minute presentation, and he wasn't going to cut anything out in order to make his point.

Every picture tells a story. In fact, a picture is worth a thousand words. But in Andy-speak, he doesn't need many words. You can tell by what he points out, how he explains why and the tone of his voice. "Somethin' ain't right here – can you see it?"

He gets on a roll moves from picture to picture, describing the deficiencies and risks associated with every single one. He moved through dozens of scenarios that make your head spin. Few questions come in as everybody takes it all in from the Jedi Master.

There is a picture, for example, where a worker ties off with a rope secured by three nails on a plank. Andy says, "Can those three nails hold 200 pounds of weight?!?!?"

His blood pressure was elevated with each passing picture that had something unsafe, while occasionally, we would see one that was right. But you started to wonder.

As each image flashed on the screen, with each brief description of another serious risk, you had to ask yourself, "How could this happen?"

Where was leadership? How could this many pictures be taken on just one large worksite? How could this be? Dozens of people could have been seriously injured, including fatalities, if they weren't lucky.

Finally, Andy laid it out for the team. This string of poor judgment by the sub-contractor led to their owner being informed they were being taken off the worksite plain and simple. They had created so much risk for their employees and those working with them that it could not be tolerated anymore.

Andy still has the "fire in the belly" when it comes to leaders holding up their end of the bargain. Keep this in mind when you feel overwhelmed by leaders who want to avoid doing what they are supposed to do.

The Punchline

If you're in the safety industry, these stories are some of the many you'll come across — and they all go right back to the failure of leadership. Somebody decided it wasn't important enough. They ignored all the advice, warnings and genuine concerns until it cost them a valuable job, their reputation and even loss of life.

In the end, no matter how you have personally witnessed both good and bad safety leadership, you begin to see a pattern. The leadership difference between the two is as simple as night and day. No sugar coating it. One approach is setting the foundation for long-term safety success; the other is just asking for trouble.

Turning a Bad Situation into Something Good

As noted earlier, our co-owner Tim Sheehan, spent part of his leadership career in the RV industry. He relates this story about a safety leadership breakthrough he witnessed in the industry.

Tim met with an RV manufacturing leader after leaving the industry and getting into safety consulting. He had a lot of safety questions when we started talking. He wanted to know in more detail what kind of safety services OECS offered, what type of clients we worked with and what strategies we were using to get leadership's attention when it came to safety. Frankly, he'd asked far more questions than our typical prospective client.

As it turns out, he had a lot on his mind when it came to safety. He had previously held a job as an executive at a large manufacturer. They had a well-defined safety plan and track record to back it up. However, during the first leg of his tenure at his current organization, he was assured they had an excellent safety culture. But he wasn't convinced. Unable to put his finger on it, things progressed as usual.

As he finished asking questions, he began to open up and share his story. The company had been in business since the 1950s. This amazing company had also accomplished something special over that period: Not one work-related fatality in over 60 years and counting.

All that came to an end when he received a phone call early one morning a few years earlier. The manager at one of his factories was calling him franticly about an incident that had just happened. An employee was struck by a forklift and was pronounced dead by paramedics.

He was absolutely heartbroken that a fatality could happen on his watch. How could this happen when he was assured the company culture was solid on safety, rarely a severe injury and no fatalities in the company's history. Even more humbling later, he had to sit across the table from the employee's two daughters and explain how this happened.

It's these circumstances, as unfortunate as they were, that became his organization's catalyst for change.

Catalyst Drives Commitment

He went on to describe what became a very tough journey of soul searching for his company and ultimately the RV industry. He dug in. Talked in-depth with the team, line level workers, dove into safety data for all their locations and began to get a clear picture of what was going on.

The data was suggesting something was amiss. Yes, while the organization had much to be proud of over the years related to their safety performance, something serious had taken grip.

It crept in slowly. It started at the edges, worked its invisible force into leadership and ultimately down through the ranks. It was infecting all facets of operations, training and so on.

The Opposite of Commitment — Complacency

Complacency had set in. Complacency had gradually altered a once-proud safety culture to the point where it was possible for the unthinkable to happen. At 6:30 am on a typical Thursday, a co-worker ran over another with a forklift, and the victim would not live to see another day, altering the employee's daughters' lives forever, along with the lives of his grandkids, his co-workers and even his community.

Even though my friend thought this was likely a problem isolated to his organization. He was on a mission to be as transparent as possible with his employees and peers throughout the industry.

He was willing to share what he learned about his own company if it would help them prevent the same tragic event that hit his company.

He attended an RV industry leadership event where pertinent topics for the industry were presented and discussed. He asked if he could share what he learned about what took place at his plant.

He went through in detail what he learned was really going on within his own company. He further pointed out that he came to some very pointed lessons that called out his own leadership and that of his team for allowing this to happen. He described precisely how complacency had crept in and taken hold.

Driving Industry Change

He went on to wonder aloud – what does the rest of the industry look like under the same microscope? What could I learn from them? Is this a wise thing to do at this time, given that these leaders are also my competitors? He wrestled with these questions and decided to go out and share it with them regardless. He felt strongly that it was the right thing to do.

To his great surprise, he discovered that his company was not alone. His leadership and transparency helped other leaders in the industry open up about their concerns, too. They all had experienced severe injuries and many near-misses getting their attention. The fatality at his facility put an exclamation point on it. They agreed to share their data with him to help form a comprehensive view of the entire industry.

From there, the data could be shared to better educate the entire RV industry and open the door for competitors to share best practices in safety, hopefully helping them all avoid the painful journey that his company had to endure.

Now, his story illustrates a strong commitment to safety. But it took a catalyst that energized his commitment. What can you draw on from your experience to deepen your commitment to safety?

Bringing Great Safety Leadership to Your Organization

Bringing outstanding safety leadership to your organization takes several vital elements. Getting those at the top engaged is essential. Continuing to build your skills through life-long learning is undoubtedly needed, as is building your network to help with all your safety challenges. Here's further insight into making that happen.

Get Leadership at the Top Engaged on Safety

First, seek out a partner for all your safety efforts. Depending on the size of your company, it might be the owner, president, VP, director, or the highest level that you can access. The higher up the organization's chain of command, the better you'll be able to access resources and get things moving forward.

Second, maybe there's a catalyst that shouldn't be squandered or lost over time but instead used as a launchpad for activating and building a strong safety culture. This could be a serious safety incident at your company. An OSHA visit that didn't go well. Concerned employees bringing up their safety-related issues with leadership. Or a workers comp insurance premium that skyrockets because of all these issues colliding together.

Third, take the time to educate leadership. You may have leaders who want to make a difference in the organization's safety efforts, but they are unsure how to get involved. It could very well be explaining to them the business case for safety and how that could make all the difference in the world. It's important to meet them where they are and discuss the key issues that are important to them, including the financial impact. We will cover the Business Case for Safety in more detail in Chapter 7, to arm you with the facts.

Integrate Safety Throughout the Organization

Discuss with leadership ways that safety can get integrated into everything your organization does. Create the time on your leadership's agenda to work through the issues. As safety becomes part of the DNA of your organization, you'll find the company will reap the enormous benefits that come with, having a strong safety culture, including a reduction in injuries and illness, better employee retention, increased cost savings and improved bottom-line growth!

OECS uses the Entrepreneurial Operating System (EOS) to run the company. Co-owner, Chris Naylor, is also an Expert EOS Implementer, having integrated this business management system into over 100 companies throughout the Midwest. Several OECS clients run their companies on EOS, too. See **https://www.eosworldwide.com/chris-naylor** for more information.

Based on the book *TRACTION* by Gino Wickman, the EOS system organizes the entire company around a set of business tools and a meeting pulse that ensures topics like safety get the attention and focus they need. In short, EOS does three main things: VISION, TRACTION, HEALTHY!

- **VISION.** Getting everyone in or organization 100% on the same page with where you're going and how you plan to get there.
- **TRACTION.** Instilling focus, discipline and accountability through the company so that everyone executes on that vision – every day!
- **HEALTHY.** Helping your leaders become a more cohesive, functional, healthy leadership team. And as we know, as the leadership team goes, so does the rest of the company!

With a system like EOS, safety is not a one-time bolt-on effort. It becomes a prominent part of everything you do. Ideally, it is part of your core values. It's something that is regularly discussed from the top on down. It's also part of recruiting team members and even how you market your company.

If this resonates with you, pick up the book *TRACTION*. You can apply the principles to running your department or your safety committee. Better yet, give a copy to your business owners or leaders and share an approach that could improve the entire organization – from better revenue and bottom-line growth to improved recruitment, retention, job satisfaction and productivity.

Note that any safety initiatives do not need to stand on their own within an organization. They should be an integral part of any program to improve quality, efficiency, productivity, or whatever. It all needs to work together to improve the performance of the organization.

Other examples that fit with safety initiatives are continuous improvement programs, lean processes or six-sigma. They all work together to eliminate waste and build superb processes.

Fuel Your Own Life-Long Learning Passion

At OECS, one of the core values is Safety Excellence. This core value includes developing a passion for safety, putting forth the effort to acquire extensive education and certifications, working on presentations skills, acquiring real-life industry experience and being a life-longer learner!

As a safety leader, it's vital to steadily "chip away" at acquiring the knowledge and insights to do your job effectively. Many of our associates have taken this approach – the long view – and have been rewarded with the fruits of their efforts down the road. Maybe this is measured by acquiring a CHST, OHST or CSP certification.

CHST stands for Construction Health and Safety Technician®. It requires three years of experience and passing a comprehensive exam. The CSP stands for Certified Safety Professional®. It requires a bachelor's degree, four years of experience and passing the CSP exam. It also requires a Board of Certified Safety Professionals® qualified credential ranging from Associate Safety Professional to Graduate Safety Professional and several other credentials.

For others, it may be how to lead and manage people more effectively. Whatever the case, commit to making yourself better at succeeding with your safety responsibilities.

For OECS, all this starts during the interview process when we ask people about our core values. We tell them upfront that adhering to our values helps us determine who to hire, fire, review, reward and recognize. We check for fit to see if they will be aligned with our company's value system.

As to life-long learning, the fact that you have this book in your sights says something about you. Even if somebody said, you had to read it! You're doing it. That puts you ahead of most right there.

A commitment to life-long learning — trying to figure out the formula that's going to ultimately put your company on track to build and sustain a strong safety culture — is what will make the difference for you and your entire organization.

This never-ending passion for learning, being a student of the safety game and bringing into the mix more and more ideas, advice, guidance and tools to accomplish your goals is what will help you get there.

Consider including some of the many safety podcasts and webinars in the market today, as well as books available to listen to during your commute. Podcasts, book apps and YouTube videos offer a treasure trove of content. You can also go "live" with local and national conferences along with associations in your area that provide great ways to learn and jump-start our next piece of advice: Networking.

Keep in mind that this is a marathon, not a sprint. Just one or two hours a week can add up to weeks of learning during that calendar year!

Build Your Network and Talk to Them

It can be hard to initiate reaching out to build relationships that bear fruit over time if you're an introvert. It can be uncomfortable, even intimidating, to stick your hand out and introduce yourself. That's the easy part. It's what comes next that can be challenging.

There are several ways to build your networking skills. But as with anything new, it's essential to identify the benefits. This can then help your motivation to overcome your reluctance to try something new.

Here are the positive benefits of networking.

- Exchange ideas with different people with a variety of backgrounds and experiences.
- Open new opportunities and possibilities with new people, new organizations and different industries.
- Develop a resource library of information based on your new contacts.
- Reach out to support others at all levels of the organization and industry.
- Gain support for your own efforts from others at all levels.
- Develop long-lasting relationships with a wide range of people.
- Grow in status and self-confidence and help others grow as well.

If that sounds good, how do you do it?

The *Harvard Business Review* article, Learn to Love Networking, recommends four strategies to become more motivated and effective at building relationships:

1. **Focus on learning**. Networking is an opportunity for discovery, not a chore.
2. **Identify common interests**. Look for ways your goals align with the goals of those you meet.
3. **Think broadly about what you can give**. You can offer knowledge, gratitude, recognition and a listening ear when that's needed.
4. **Find a higher purpose**. Think about the benefits to your organization or even your industry.

All too often, we think about networking from the perspective of "What's in it for me?" Instead, it needs to begin with how you can help others. It's the law of giving where everything flows from that natural beginning point, and the benefits build over time to everyone in the relationship.

Keith Ferrazzi, in the book, *Never Eat Alone,* has this great quote:

"The more people you help, the more help you'll have and the more help you'll have helping others."

Networking is one more part of your leadership skill set. It can help provide information and the support you need to advance your safety goals. But the building part must happen first, and it needs to happen continuously. It all starts with finding ways to help others.

To get you started in building your network, identify your company's membership in trade associations. They offer an opening to connect with others in your industry. Learn how you can get involved and, therefore, tap their network and resources.

Another approach is to utilize a social media platform like LinkedIn. You can search out experts through your existing network and make connections you never thought possible. You may even find that others are connecting with you to gain insight into industry issues. Remember, it's about helping others.

Commitment — Summary

That's a brief insight into the first of the 5 C's of Safety, Commitment. Of course, that's also driven by leadership and ultimately at every level of an organization that's focused on safety.

- The first C stands for **COMMITMENT**!
- Commitment starts at the top. All roads lead back to Leadership — and that includes YOU! It's time you took on the mantle of safety leadership.
- Is there a CATALYST that you can put to good use to drive your organization's safety commitment?
- Take stock of the differences between great leaders and bad leaders. Great leaders build a safety program from the ground up and lead by example. Bad leaders are the "no shows" who create safety risks by inaction.
- Do you ever hear, "That's never happened here?" Think long and hard about the RV industry story. It happened there after a 60-year record.
- A life-long learning passion for safety can be fueled by taking courses, reading books, listening to podcasts, attending conferences and so much more. Along with that comes networking with those in your industry as

well as local leaders to help provide insight when you need it.

- Consider learning more about the EOS system and pick up the book *TRACTION* by Gino Wickman. See **https://www.eosworldwide.com/chris-naylor** or reach out to Chris directly at **chris.naylor@eosworldwide.com** for more information.
- Visit **oecscomply.com** for more information on this topic.

Is complacency lurking in the background at your company? Remember, "Procrastination is the assassin of motivation." It's time to get started on your company's safety journey.

Chapter 4 — Compliance: Setting the Foundation

"A prudent man foresees the difficulties ahead and prepares for them; the simpleton goes blindly on and suffers the consequences."

— Proverbs 22:3

Gary's Forklift Training

Gary had joined OECS after 30 years in the Army. He did many jobs while serving our country, and they were often met with the same focus and energy on display at our client's facility in the Twin Cities.

Gary was new to his safety associate role and was conducting forklift certification for the client's new employees.

During the training, he quizzed the group on properly operating the forklift. He had pictures that helped illustrate how difficult it was to see pedestrians when in the seat of the forklift. He had them take a written exam. He reviewed each question after the fact to make sure they got it right and understood why.

Then he brought them out onto the shop floor, had them demonstrate they knew the controls and then get in, put on their seat belt, of course maneuver the unit down the aisle and back. All standard stuff when you're doing the training the way it is supposed to be done.

At the end of the process, one of the participants brought something up with Gary. "I worked down the street for ten years. We never had any training or anybody really paying attention to what you went through with us today. And no wonder we had so many problems! Guys were ramming into things and almost running people over constantly."

He went on to say how the difference in the two safety cultures was obvious to him, and he was glad he made the move to his new company. "They care," he said.

And that's what this is all about—using the motivation for getting into and staying in compliance as a springboard into action. Following a plan. Training the team on the basic requirements and getting hands-on. This is something that Gary was accustomed to doing after spending years in the military, where all too often situations are life or death!

OSHA Investigators Reflect Back

Over the years, OECS has benefited from working with several former Minnesota OSHA investigators and consultants on their team. They've visited hundreds of general industry and construction sites. Some as part of an ongoing scheduled set of visits, some in response to an incident or complaint.

When asked about their first impressions upon entering the business or construction site and what it taught them, their response was interesting.

They described essentially what an excellent visit looks like versus a bad one. For example, they encountered receptionists who were prepared and professional about their entry versus those who simply panicked. They described what initially appeared to be a very organized, well-oiled machine to something on the other end of the spectrum, a disaster in the making.

All of it, each description, started to paint a picture. They would say, "It didn't take long to get a sense of what a company's safety culture was all about from how they initially greeted you, how the leader behaved, to how their safety materials were organized, how training was documented, initial impressions on general housekeeping and so on. Eye-opening."

It's hard to imagine a company is really committed to building a strong safety culture when the compliance portion of the equation, so critical to setting the foundation, is not in place.

Why Compliance is Foundational to Safety

There are all too many books that would now begin to delve into the details of the four major OSHA standards, depending on what industry is relevant for you. Well, that's not going to happen in this book. After all, the details are all available to you online.

Instead, at this stage, this book will establish meaningful context for these standards. Then it will look at why compliance to these standards is so critical to establishing a strong foundation on which you can build your safety culture!

Andy Smoka is an OECS safety associate who spent 28 years with Minnesota OSHA as a Senior Consultant. He helped write several OSHA standards still in effect today.

When Andy visits the office, you must stop what you're doing and listen! He has so many stories and insights to share that you never hear the same story twice. In addition to his many years with OSHA, Andy served 31 years in the Navy as Commander Master Chief and another nine years in the U.S. Army as a Commander Sergeant Major. Andy is 74 years old and goes for 10-mile hikes weekly to keep in "game shape."

Andy has one of the most clear and compelling views on safety compliance. Plus, he can draw on many stories to illustrate his points.

Where the Rubber Meets the Road

"I pulled onto a job site one day," Andy begins to say. "They were building a 5-story office tower. I could see they were without the proper safety equipment – not just in a couple of areas but also throughout the project. When I engaged with the workers, they really didn't understand what the regulations were. More importantly, they didn't understand the why's behind them."

Andy found the supervisor responsible for the work being done on the site. He quizzed him on several issues he saw and realized the supervisor had no idea, either. In fact, he had a great deal of resistance to hearing the message.

Andy said he took a deep breath and walked the supervisor through the three major unnecessary risks his workers were taking. He went through each one to explain the implications of their actions if something went amiss and how the OSHA regulations were designed to help avoid this.

Andy explained, "When you go back in time and look at how the OSHA regulations came to be, it's evident why. The government was hearing a tremendous outcry from the spouses of lost workers! For the most part, wives lived with the aftermath of husbands being lost on the job. Before 1970 when OSHA was formed, there was very little worker protection.

"Think of it this way. The original OSHA regulations came into existence during an incredible upheaval in our country. The Vietnam War was raging. Republicans and Democrats were divided on this and many other issues facing our country. However, even in the face of these times, both parties joined forces and compromised to establish safety regulations and a department to enforce them. Their legacy has saved thousands of lives."

Another point Andy drives home is how much further everyone needs to go. "Even today, when you compare the number of deaths on construction sites across the country versus the number of soldiers lost in the Afghanistan War, you'll be surprised to know that more deaths happen on the construction sites! The difference is that soldiers prepare for the strong possibility of death.

"The OSHA codes have evolved over the years. This evolution is data-driven. OSHA responds to data, looking in the rear-view mirror of worker fatalities to adjust their approach. This could mean strengthening/clarifying existing regulations or adding new ones."

Andy's career with OSHA was at the forefront of implementing these regulations and holding business leaders accountable. OSHA soon realized that many business leaders and workers did not understand the regulations. In some cases, it was not clear how to effectively translate the intent of the regulations to actionable change at the job site or plant. Something emerged out of this stage that has had a long-lasting positive impact on OSHA and their relationship with business: OSHA consulting support was born.

From this realization, OSHA formed a training for the first group of consultants to go out into the field. Andy was among them. He could quickly see what needed to be done. "Nobody knew what the rules were. I started to roll up my sleeves and ask businesses for their safety programs. On several big projects in the Twin Cities, there were significant gaps in the programs and planning. This is where I figured we could be of tremendous help to reduce fatalities.

"The other element missing from the equation in the early days was training. Since the rules were not clear to leadership, no training took place covering the regulations. The value OSHA consultation could provide businesses, and frankly, the seeds of the safety training industry came out of this stage.

"Training emerged as the single greatest lever we had at that time and still today. Without clear regulations that can be translated into trainable segments, it will remain a mystery to the worker."

Through many years of experience, seeing the painful outcomes of when proper procedures and training are absent, Andy emphasizes this point about compliance. "We need to be clear where the ultimate accountability lies for being in compliance. This is where in construction, for example, to this day, owners of contracting or sub-contracting companies still point their fingers back at each other. Clearly understanding where the ultimate accountability for worker safety rests is critical to this entire discussion. When it's clear, smart leaders will take action and address the safety issues requiring their attention. When it's fuzzy, eventually bad things can happen."

The 60% Solution?

It's not uncommon for leaders to get frustrated at times when it comes to having to be in compliance with a daunting list of safety regulations. Some will believe that the expectations are too cumbersome for their workers to follow and be productive at the same time, or they are unnecessary altogether.

When asked how high the bar is set in meeting the current regulations, Andy responds this way. "The fact is the bar is at about 60% of where it needs to be. After years of working with these regulations, with businesses and their workers and seeing the outcomes with injuries and fatalities – that's about right. I've seen first-hand the gap that exists with fall protection, for example, comparing the regulations versus best practices is a big difference. This is where leaders can move their company to the next level. Compliance is the table stakes, the price of admission, whatever you want to call it. Ultimately building a strong safety culture is where you get to the next level."

Are We "Wired" for Compliance?

For almost 30 years, OECS has been helping clients interpret the complex nature of OSHA standards and translate the intent of the regulations into actionable change. They learned that there are some key attributes every safety leader should keep in mind to be successful at navigating the complexities of OSHA compliance.

As Andy mentioned earlier, those responsible for safety could become quite frustrated with the daunting list of safety regulations. To dig in further, Chris Naylor, co-owner of OECS, introduced the team to the Kolbe Strengths Assessment.

The Kolbe measures how people instinctively take action to accomplish their goals at work. These strengths – or "striving instincts" – are hard-wired, do not vary by gender, age, race, or geography and are unchanging over time!

The Kolbe categorizes strengths in four domains and measures them on a scale of 1-10. There are no terrible scores, only different strengths.

- **FactFinder.** The instinctive way we gather and share information – from a very high-level overview to a super detailed analysis.
- **FollowThru.** The instinctive way we organize, from unstructured to super systemized.
- **QuickStart.** The instinctive way we deal with risk and uncertainty, from seeking to stabilize to being comfortable with a high degree of risk and change.
- **Implementor.** The instinctive way we handle space and tangibles, from dealing in subjectives to doing our best work hands-on.

The scoring for the Kolbe assessment is broken into:

1-3 – CounterActing (or stabilizing) Strengths
4-6 – Mediating Strengths (bridging the extremes)
7-10 – Initiating Strengths (leading with this action)

Applying this to safety, the Implementor strength is very relevant to the people who attend many of our trainings. If they accomplish their work best being hands-on or if they're highly mechanical – like in the construction and manufacturing fields – they might have a score of 7-10.

On the other hand, leaders typically have CounterActing Implementer scores of 1-3 – dealing mostly in subjectives – like ideas, values, concepts and vision. With such different ways of looking at the world and accomplishing goals, one can see that communications and training disconnects are inevitable unless they understand these dynamics!

With all OECS safety associates taking this assessment, a strong pattern emerged over time. Chris marveled at how similar the top safety associates' scores were – usually high on FactFinder and FollowThru, with stabilizing or counteracting scores on QuickStart and a variety of scores for Implementor.

She also noticed how different the business owners' QuickStart scores were (Tim 7, Chris 9) in comparison to the associates (usually between 1-3). "We could see why at times, we would become frustrated — and they with us as we would push ahead with this change or that," Chris said.

Keep in mind the Kolbe isn't a panacea for selecting safety professionals — but it can be a pretty darn good indicator of success. One must also consider the "whole person," their unique experience, as well as the cognitive (IQ), emotional intelligence (EQ) and personality. With that said, here are the benefits of utilizing this assessment:

Individual
- Improve Efficiency and Productivity
- Develop Leaders and Managers
- Increase Engagement and Job Satisfaction

Team
- Enhance Communication
- Collaborate Effectively
- Boost Performance
- Improve Team Health

Organization
- Hire and Retain Successfully/Maximize "Fit"
- Right People in Right Role
- Amplify Culture
- Improve Organizational Results

Seeing is Believing

One OECS safety associate, Amy Hardwood, exemplifies the high FactFinder Strength described above. This strength has often driven her to ask that extra set of questions that others would not. Countless times, she's shown that rolling up your sleeves and going on a mission to find out the facts on behalf of your clients will move everyone to the best conclusion. It's just like peeling an onion.

But the complimentary strength Amy possesses is FollowThru. She's organized, focused and wired to take the insight she has on a safety issue – and see it through! The combination of these strengths is powerful in the safety world.

Tim O'Connor and Mark Shields also epitomize the value that FactFinders can bring to a company. When COVID hit the U.S., OECS scrambled like everyone else to determine how this would impact their clients.

Both Tim and Mark did ongoing in-depth research to continually provide OECS associates and clients with the information they needed. They helped prioritize and sort out the information from many sites and sources to formulate a clear point of view – constantly balancing CDC guidance with federal, state and local level mandates as well as OSHA standards. They helped make the trade-offs when dealing with the many gray areas related to COVID along the way while at the same time backing their work up with solid evidence.

Utilizing tools like the Kolbe can help a leader determine if they have the right person in the right seat – in this case, finding someone who is wired for safety implementation and execution. A winning combination is someone high in FactFinder, strong in

FollowThru, counteracting in QuickStart and mediating in Implementor!

For more information, see **www.kolbe.com** or reach out to Chris Naylor at **chris@oecscomply.com**.

The Proven Process Right Under Our Noses

For each of the C's, OECS believes that not only the right mindset and strengths are imperative but so is having a process to follow. How else can you get traction toward improving outcomes without having a roadmap to follow?

Having a clear, proven process illustrates how your company delivers on its promise. It sets the foundation.

Nearly 30 years ago, the founder of OECS developed and followed a proven process. The new version was illustrated, in classic continuous improvement form, the exact order things would take place with a new client. Once the OECS Proven Process was launched, it would become continuous from month-to-month, quarter-to-quarter and year-to-year.

By the way, Tim Peterson from OECS tells the story this way: "We had this process we followed with our clients for years. When our new owners started working with us, they said, 'Hey, that's a Proven Process!' Together we updated and tweaked it and continue to use it as part of everything we do."

As you walk through the OECS Proven Process, you can see why each part is crucial to tackling the compliance part of the equation effectively.

The OECS Proven Process

A process is critical to achieving consistent results time and time again. Without a process, you're required to create a method of solving a problem every single time you encounter one. Since the variety of problems that surface is almost never-ending, you'll need to rethink how best to solve the latest one that lands in your lap.

Instead, a proven process that is followed time and again helps you take all the necessary steps to resolve the issue successfully. Nothing is left out or forgotten along the way. It simply builds success upon success.

Here are the key details of the OECS Proven Process. You can apply this process internally if you have experienced safety professionals. However, a "new set of eyes" can be very helpful to get a firm idea of where you really stand relative to others in your

industry. A partnership with both internal and external expertise helps ensure the company's safety goals are met.

Assess

This part of the OECS Proven Process requires the appropriate safety expertise. In your case, this could be outside expertise, like a safety consultant from OECS or OSHA consultation, to provide an honest assessment of the current state of your safety plan and culture.

This is like having an accounting firm check what your accountant is doing. It must be done on-site, evaluating the quality of your safety programs, walking the facility or job site, interacting and talking with the employees – to truly get a good assessment of where things stand before taking any action. Here are the key steps in simple terms.

- Get to know the company.
- Understand the safety needs.
- Evaluate the facility and/or job site.
- Determine the gaps in safety efforts.
- Review safety programs.
- Identify if there are needs for industrial hygiene and environmental health.

Develop

Once you have a good baseline assessment of your company's safety plan, it's now time to develop or evolve a new or updated plan to bring your team to the next level. Here are the key steps.

- Create a customized safety action plan.
- Check for compliance with all OSHA regulations.
- Work together to make this happen.

- Structure safety responsibilities at all levels in the organization, ensuring accountabilities are clearly understood.

OECS takes great pride in customizing safety programs and plans for clients. But with so many different programs, the range in size of client organizations and the uniqueness of each – the process quickly becomes complex. That's where Anita Erickson came in, OECS's Operations Coordinator, and developed a program database to help manage this.

She explained, "We really had to scrub each program template to update them and make sure they were current with OSHA regulations, before we can even begin to customize the program for clients. There is a lot at stake for these companies. These programs and plans reflect who is ultimately accountable for what goes on safety-wise in the company." This stage of the OECS Proven Process is a critical piece to the safety puzzle.

Implement

Once the plan is in place, it's almost like "nothing to it but to do it." If only it were that simple. It's always a matter of providing the skills needed through training and then following up to measure progress. Here's how we've defined this critical step in the process.

- Provide training.
- Create safety programs.
- Conduct safety audits.
- Work side-by-side on implementation activities.
- Be accessible 24/7/365.
- Build a strong safety culture.

OECS has learned over the years that there is no shortcut for implementation. Scott Bertrand, CST, a construction safety associate for OECS, highlighted the importance of this during a recent visit to a client's job site. While auditing a car dealership remodel for the second time in a month, he noticed something different.

"Last time I was here," Scott said, "they were hanging from the second story without being properly tied-off! I approached the worker and reminded him about the proper way to safely work at this height and how to complete the task at hand efficiently. I also reminded him about the consequences of falling from two stories. He listened, and now the second time around, he's implementing the plan properly." Scott went on to say, "If you're not inspecting what you expect, you'll find safety gaps!"

Train

This step is so important. You can put posters up all over the workplace, but they can become meaningless unless the organization puts training behind every single initiative. People need to see the commitment, and they need to know precisely what they need to do to match the organizational commitment. Here are the key steps.

- Deliver customized training with polished presenters.
- Engage all employees.
- Use easy-to-understand content.
- Provide onsite training and/or virtual training on-demand to reach all employees.

Kelli J. Chromey, Ph.D., leads our Learning Management System (LMS) training, called On Demand. With thousands of participants on the OECS LMS system, she sees first-hand how companies use a combination of strategies to engage their employees in safety training.

As companies evolve to embrace both in-person and online technology, today's employees appreciate the flexibility and commitment it shows from their employers. "You can tell when a company fully grasps how to use different approaches and tools to get their safety training across. I can see it in the companies where participation is high, and comprehension scores through our knowledge checks are strong. It says a lot about that company's grasp of this important part of the overall process."

Support

Delivering on a safety plan can be quite an extensive effort. Yet it could easily fall apart if there is not continuing support to address each issue as it arises and make adjustments as needed. Here's what is critical for supporting any organization and its safety efforts.

- Provide written safety audits to help gauge progress.
- Attend safety committee meetings.
- Review the EMR/300 log.
- Help reinforce building a safety culture.
- Be OSHA ready.

Great, all done, right? Not really. There's a reason the process is illustrated as a circle. It all needs to start again to keep pushing your safety efforts to new heights.

When the Process Pays Off

One of the more unnerving experiences for OECS clients is when OSHA shows up one morning at their door. Often, it's part of their "programmed visit" plan. The industries with higher incident rates and issues often get put on the radar. Then the OSHA investigators are assigned to make their rounds accordingly. It's not uncommon for most businesses within specific industries with higher incident rates to get visited every three years.

As an example, one morning, a call came in from a frantic client. "OSHA IS HERE!" As part of client support, a safety associate will travel to the site to walk alongside the client and the OSHA Investigator during the visit. Our associate, Mark Shields, who was available at the time, made his way over to the client's location as fast as he could.

After the visit, Mark recounted the inspection results. "Well, I think it went well. They got ZERO citations!" Having an OSHA Investigator walk through your facility for a couple of hours and not find anything warranting a citation is, in fact, a significant accomplishment.

Mark went on to describe how this outcome transpired. "A lot of hard work on behalf of the client – their entire team, myself and a little luck, to be quite honest. But don't get me wrong, this didn't happen by accident."

He went on to say, "They really bought into the fundamentals – they stuck with the process. Evaluating the issues, implementing their safety action plan, providing training on the topics that keep them in compliance, reading through and acting on the safety audits I provided them, supporting their Safety Committee and more. They have really bought into setting and maintaining a solid safety foundation. I'm proud of the progress we've made."

Mark's story says so much about the importance of applying a process that enables companies to get themselves in safety compliance—ultimately positioning them with the foundation necessary to continue the journey by strengthening their safety culture.

Compliance — Summary

Following a proven process can help bring you and your organization into compliance and keep you there. But it does take time and effort.

- The second C stands for **COMPLIANCE!**
- Compliance is the foundation of safety. Operating without following sound safety practices puts everyone at risk. Training is a big part of making this happen.
- The OECS Proven Process includes assessing, developing, implementing, training and supporting. When followed closely and repeatedly, it gets your safety program where it needs to be and keeps it there. Visit **oecscomply.com** for a visual example of the OECS Proven Process.
- Understanding the context of the OSHA regulations is an important starting point as a safety leader. OSHA has tremendous and committed people focused on safety. Everyone can learn from them.
- What type of talent does it take to succeed in the Compliance portion of the 5 C's of Safety? Kolbe assessments have taught us to find people on your team who are "wired" for this crucial task.

Chapter 5 — Culture: Building a Strong Safety Culture

"Safety is not an intellectual exercise to keep us in work. It is a matter of life and death. It is the sum of our contributions to safety management that determines whether the people we work with live or die."

— Sir Brian Appleton, CBE awarded in 2002 for his services to safety management

Safety 24/7 – Building an Incident-Free Culture

The team at OECS values greatly the book written by Greg Anderson and Robert L. Lorber, Ph.D. – *Safety 24/7 Building an Incident-Free Culture.* It really hits the mark in helping leaders get up to speed quickly on behavioral-based safety. The short stories help reveal basic concepts and bring them home. The book resonated with our team and our clients. It was immediately relatable. We highly recommend it as part of your safety arsenal.

OECS Lead Safety Associate, Melissa Olheiser, from our Fargo, North Dakota office, took it a step further. She envisioned working with our more evolved clients on a whole process to take it from "read this book," to let's read it, talk about it and act on each chapter.

Melissa explained her approach this way. "I'd meet with the client beforehand to understand what they wanted to accomplish with their Safety 24/7 plan. We talked about their goals and what content or topic would be appropriate for their audience. This understanding really helped shape my approach with them."

As Melissa went through her process, it became apparent that the upfront meeting and then assigning the book for all participants to read was just the beginning.

"Then we roll up our sleeves and go through discussing each chapter, each of the key concepts within the chapter and what roadblocks or issues they might encounter along the way. We apply the EOS process, build our issues list, work through each issue and ultimately assign to-do items or next steps for each participant. This isn't a presentation or download; this is a working session," she said with excitement!

"One session builds on the other, usually one to two hours long each month, all toward the greater goal of making sure their teams go home safe every night!"

She went on to say that companies that go through this process with her are always astounded at the eventual outcome. As they reflect on the starting point, they are always amazed by the progress they make by staying focused and using the working sessions to build momentum and take action.

This is one example of how a company's commitment to building a strong safety culture, paired with a capable facilitator, can really move the dial. There is so much to this culture topic it warrants a deeper dive.

The Plain, Uncomplicated and Complicated Reality About Culture

When studying about culture, it's like peeling back the layers of the onion, so to speak, so you can begin to understand how to reshape culture. The reward is when you sense the actions you're taking as a leader impact your organization's culture.

However, building a strong culture is elusive. When you look at how the experts define culture, you'll be surprised to find no precise alignment on even the definition, much less on what steps to take to do the required work.

Culture is like electricity – it's invisible yet controlled and transferred.

A classic definition of company culture is a set of shared values, goals, attitudes and behaviors that characterize an organization. A strong company culture attracts and retains better talent — that means lower turnover, fewer new hires and better productivity and cohesion among the team.

With culture, there's an enormous opportunity for leadership to strengthen it.

First, study up, do your homework and become a student on the topic. Then use your instincts; it doesn't have to be overly complicated. This is where the exercise of defining what, from your own experiences, defines a great culture versus a poor one.

That's right. You were likely part of a healthy culture at some point in your life, easily contrasted against the time when you were part of one that was not so good.

Here's a quick summary of experts on culture who may be helpful as you start to delve into improving your safety culture. Review these options and decide which one would be best for you to pursue in more detail.

Culture Trumps Everything

Gustavo R. Grodnitzky, Ph.D., in his book, *Culture Trumps Everything,* laid out a simple way for us to envision exactly what he meant by the title of his book.

"Saying that culture trumps everything means that if employees within your organization are goal-orientated, team-focused and driven by performance, it is because your culture demands it. Conversely, if your organization has employees that don't care about goals, don't care about teams and don't care about performance, it is because your culture allows that, as well.

"It is essential to understand that culture is very much like a garden. Left unattended, a garden will grow all sorts of weeds and plants that you have no interest in growing, and that will choke out the fruits, the vegetables and the flowers you do want to grow.

"But, if you spent time in the garden – if you spend time on your culture – and you go through picking out the weeds and plants you don't want to grow, it becomes a lot easier to grow the fruits, the vegetables and the flowers you do want to grow."

Gustavo went on further to say in his book, "Spending time in the garden of your culture means that focusing on your organizational culture is the difference between working *on* your business versus working *in* your business. Working *on* your business means working *on* your culture because culture trumps everything."

Reading his book is invaluable if you're up for really expanding your thinking on culture. Early on, he states that culture and people come before profit for the most successful companies. This, for some, is in reverse order as they see the world. But gaining deeper insights into the actual primary drivers of humans – which are to connect and belong as Gustavo points out, helps explain why.

What are the implications for you in your journey to build a strong safety culture? Think about how you and your leadership or safety team spend their time. Investing time in your "garden" will pay dividends in the short and long term.

The Culture Code

In his recent book, *The Culture Code*, Daniel Coyle outlined his findings after studying for four years what he considered to be the world's eight most successful groups. This perspective is valuable because it spans many different groups in society today.

Across these unique and different groups, he saw a pattern emerge. He found that a specific set of skills created their cultures. These skills tap into the power of our social brains to create interactions that make a difference.

These three skills provide a unique window into exactly what he saw within these eight groups.

- First, Build Safety — explores how connection signals generate a bond of belonging and identity.
- Second, Shared Vulnerability — explains how habits of mutual risk drive trusting cooperation.
- Third, Establish Purpose — tells how narratives create shared goals and values.

These three skills work together from the bottom up, first building the group connection and then channeling it into action.

"The Culture Code" is packed with insights that support the identification and cultivation of these three skills necessary to build a strong culture. The stories he draws on to help explain each component are compelling, too.

What are the implications for you in building a strong safety culture? How you manage group dynamics considering these insights will shape what kind of outcomes occur. That includes safety goals as well. Investing time to understand more about the three skills necessary for your company to make a breakthrough will pay dividends.

Winning Teams, Winning Cultures

Larry Senn, author of *"Winning Teams, Winning Cultures,"* has worked with hundreds of companies to help them embrace transformational change. He talked about the importance of culture shaping while addressing the elephant in the room.

He said, "People and organizations are creatures of habit and changing habits is much harder than changing structures or systems. It seemed to us that teams and organizations, like people, had personalities, and ignoring or not dealing with an organization's personality traits could be fatal to our change effort.

"We call this phenomenon *the jaws of culture* because cultural habits, such as resistance to change and turf issues, chew up the improvement process and reduce or eliminate the results."

Larry went on to draw a picture on the board. The first box header read, "Initiatives," and a big arrow pointed into a large set of jaws with sharp teeth labeled "Cultural Barriers," which in turn had an arrow pointing to another box labeled "Low Results."

The jaws of culture and each of the individual teeth were intended to represent turf issues, blaming and excuses, resistance to change, bureaucracy, self-interest, low level of trust and so on.

You can no doubt see this reflected in your organization. No matter how many new strategies or change initiatives that new leaders try to drive, the jaws of culture can chew them up.

What are the implications for you in your journey to build a strong safety culture? Think about the barriers that are getting in the way of a better safety culture emerging. Are there certain people, processes, procedures or gaps giving further strength to your company's "jaws of culture?" What can you do to help reduce the barriers and allow the safety initiatives to get the oxygen they deserve?

Steps to Safety Culture Excellence

Steps to Safety Culture Excellence, by Terry L. Mathis and Shawn M. Galloway, provides another insightful angle about culture. Their work lays out a detailed plan. STEPS is the acronym they use to outline – Strategic Targets for Excellent Performance in Safety™.

"The STEPS methodology suggests that we systematically and progressively assess and address each of these issues and ensure that no element of our safety culture is reinforcing risk." This book does the arduous job of practically and holistically mapping out a path to help a company achieve and sustain safety excellence.

"Most definitions of safety culture define the culture's characteristics. The definition we propose involves developing a culture's capabilities. The most basic power of a safety culture is the ability to improve. This is the real challenge; not what managers or consultants can make of a safety culture, but what a safety culture can make of itself.

"Once a culture can take a STEP toward better performance, it can continue to take STEPS until it achieves its personal best. So, the real question is not, "What is our safety culture like? But rather, "What can our safety culture do?" How do the norms of the group influence individuals within the group when they make safety decisions or follow common practices? Can the group learn to improve its own norms, common practices and the ways in which it influences members?"

This book is "meatier" on this topic than most and is a good resource for larger organizations looking for a more sophisticated playbook to follow.

So, What's the Point?

Those five sources are all worth getting your own copy, pursuing a book summary or downloading your audiobook app. Committing to life-long learning, becoming a student on culture and finding sources to give you the insight you need are all an essential part of grasping the all-important third C, Culture!

Another valuable approach is the Gallup® Q12®. This is the next section on building a strong safety culture that you will find very revealing!

What Gallup® Can Teach Us About Safety

At safety conferences, it became a common practice for speakers to reference research that Gallup® had done on employee engagement.

In short, Gallup's data essentially said that only 33% of US workers were truly "engaged." And if the majority of workers were NOT engaged, no wonder we were not making the progress we should with safety results.

Gallup would briefly talk about the relationship between engagement and safety but not go deeper than that. So, where did these numbers come from?

THE STATE OF THE AMERICAN WORKPLACE[2]

This study presents an unparalleled look into the modern workforce. The report is based on Gallup's in-depth research and was created to help business leaders optimize their attraction, retention, engagement and performance strategies in a time of extraordinary change.

The findings and best practices speak to employees' evolving wants and needs and give leaders a clear understanding of what it takes to be an exceptional workplace.

Gallup developed *State of the American Workplace* using data collected from more than 195,600 U.S. employees via the Gallup Panel and Gallup Daily tracking in 2015 and 2016 and more than 31 million respondents through Gallup's Q12 Client Database. First launched in 2010, this is the third iteration of the report.

---

[2] Gallup State of the American Workplace Report
https://www.gallup.com/workplace/238085/state-american-workplace-report-2017.aspx

More About the Q12® Survey

Gallup has surveyed people's opinions for years with their business division. Their clients include thousands of companies that roll up to millions of employees who eventually take the survey. This group has designed what they believe to be the 12 questions that, if asked annually to all employees at a company, gives leadership insight into just how engaged they are and how that is evolving.

Please note that Gallup has allowed us to publish this information to inform our readers on the detailed aspects of employee engagement and their impact on workplace safety. These questions are proprietary to Gallup. They are legally protected and can only be included in surveys conducted by Gallup.

Here's the complete list of their Q12 questions and how they are organized across basic, individual, teamwork and growth needs.

Basic Needs[3]

Q01: I know what is expected of me at work.
Q02: I have the materials and equipment I need to do my work right.
Q03: At work, I have the opportunity to do what I do best every day.

Individual Needs

Q04: In the last seven days, I have received recognition or praise for doing good work.
Q05: My supervisor, or someone at work, seems to care about me as a person.

---

[3] Q12 questions Copyright © 1993-1998 Gallup, Inc.

Q06: There is someone at work who encourages my development.

Teamwork Needs
Q07: At work, my opinions seem to count.
Q08: The mission or purpose of my company makes me feel my job is important.
Q09: My associates or fellow employees are committed to doing quality work.
Q10: I have a best friend at work.

Growth Needs[4]
Q11: In the last six months, someone at work has talked to me about my progress.
Q12: This last year, I have had opportunities at work to learn and grow.

These 12 questions then make up the core of the data set that positions Gallup to share fantastic insight into a company's quest to build a strong culture.

How Engagement is Measured

To be truly counted as engaged, survey participants had to choose a "5" on a scale of 1 to 5. Here's the scale.
- 1 – Strongly disagree
- 2 – Disagree
- 3 – Do not disagree or agree
- 4 – Agree
- 5 – Strongly agree

---

[4] Q12 questions Copyright © 1993-1998 Gallup, Inc.

In other words, to be considered an "engaged" employee, they had to answer a 5 – strongly agree – on several questions.

That sets a high bar for any company. But to better understand what this signifies, it's essential to understand a bit more about the questions being asked.

What Quartile Analysis Showed Us

Once you have the data and begin to understand the implications of your employee responses, remarkable insights into performance start to emerge.

The Gallup "secret sauce" takes the results and divides them into four quartiles. Top, second, third and bottom. There is a BIG difference between the top quartile performers versus the bottom ones. You can see, for example, gaps between the top and bottom quartiles performance ranging from 10% to 70%!

Safety Jumps Off the Page!

In preparing information for a presentation on "The Business Case for Safety" to a group of business leaders, OECS dove into the Gallup analysis on engagement. Was there more to learn through drilling down in the data that may be useful in the case for building strong safety leadership?

Sure enough, the top-quartile employee engagement companies out-performed bottom quartile companies by a wide margin across many key metrics.

But one of the results jumped off the page – top versus bottom quartile companies *experienced 70% fewer safety incidents*. That's right. Said another way, the top 25% had far fewer safety incidents than the bottom 25%. So much so that it was the most substantial improvement out of the 11 metrics tracked!

Here's a summary of the key metrics included in the *State of the American Workplace* – comparing top-quartile companies versus bottom quartile:

- 70% fewer employee safety incidents
- 41% lower absenteeism
- 28% less shrinkage
- 58% fewer patient safety incidents
- 40% fewer quality incidents
- 10% higher customer metrics
- 17% high productivity
- 20% higher sales
- 21% higher profitability
- 24% lower turnover (high-turnover organizations)
- 59% lower turnover (low-turnover organizations)

The Silver Bullet?

There it is, folks, the "answer" to what it will take to blow away any of your safety goals. That's right; it's an open book test. Just get your employees to answer "Strongly Agree" to many of the Q12 questions, and you're set. Only if it was that easy!

Digging deeper into some of the questions and the responses that drove the top quartile safety results, or "peeling the onion," can provide more actionable steps. This, in turn, can help strengthen your overall company culture, including safety.

Getting at the Basic Needs: What Do I Get?

Question #2 of the Q12 asks the survey participant to answer; I *have the materials and equipment I need to do my work right.*[5] Remember, the responses can range from strongly disagree to strongly agree.

When Gallup summarized their finding for just this question across thousands of employees, they found that 3 in 10 U.S. employees strongly agreed. Said another way, 7 in 10 could NOT answer strongly agree. What are the implications to your safety plans if this is the case at your company?

Gallup went on to say that by moving that ratio to 6 in 10 employees strongly agreeing, companies could realize an 11% increase in profitability, *a 32% reduction in safety incidents* and a 27% improvement in quality.

Of the 12 questions, this one is the strongest indicator of job stress! This is undoubtedly the place for you to pay attention as the newly minted safety leader or the one tasked with turning your safety ship around. By simply asking your employees, holding roundtable or Town Hall meetings, creating a survey focused on this topic alone, you can help provide a blueprint to moving more of your folks from a 1, 2 or 3 into the 5 response – STRONGLY AGREE!

Bob Williams, CHST, STSC, a safety associate with OECS, has seen the impact of this first-hand. This took place in the middle of discussing building a strong safety culture with a client.

"The client was asked, in front of the owner, *"Do you have the materials and equipment you need to do the job safely?"*[6] Then

---

[5] Q12 questions Copyright © 1993-1998 Gallup, Inc.

they about leaped out of their chairs! Rattling off a list of things the company had done to address this issue." Bob knew he had hit a vein. He went on to say, "No surprise that this effort is why they were in the middle of a 3+ year run with no lost days!"

Individual Needs: What do I Give?

Let's keep rolling – question #3 asks the survey participants to answer, *At work, I could do what I do best every day.*[7] Does this hit home for you? Are you able to do what you do best most of the time? Read on!

Gallup found that 4 in 10 U.S. employees strongly agree with this question. By moving this to as many as 8 in 10 employees, organizations could realize an 8% increase in customer engagement scores, a 14% increase in profitability and a *46% reduction in safety incidents*!

Working to figure out what your employees are good at and creating a way for them to do this most of the time creates a sense of purpose that has a powerful impact on a company's culture.

At OECS, we check for fit constantly. We ask our safety associates questions like – how are you doing? Is the work the kind of work that gets you energized? Are you doing what you love most of the time or just some of the time? Leaders must check in with their teams to ensure they can do what they love to do most of the time.

Teamwork: Do I Belong Here?

---

[6] Q12 questions Copyright © 1993-1998 Gallup, Inc.
[7] Q12 questions Copyright © 1993-1998 Gallup, Inc.

Question #7 – *At work, my opinions seem to count.*[8] This one may seem a bit more nuanced than the other questions. However, taking the time to hear people out when they have issues or concerns is important. It doesn't mean, in this case, you act on all the input you receive. What's critical is that people feel heard, and the appropriate action takes place where it makes sense.

Just 3 in 10 U.S. employees strongly agree with this question. By moving that ratio to 6 in 10 employees, companies could realize a 27% reduction in turnover, *a 40% reduction in safety incidents* and a 12% increase in productivity!

Sometimes being a leader can be a lonely job. The fact is that no one person has all the answers. So why not ask, seek out and encourage your employees to give input on all matters involving how your company can get better – including safety?

Lead Safety Associate, Mark Shields, was conducting training for a client. At the end, he solicited questions and input about the topic he had just covered.

One of the employees sitting in the back said, "What do you mean management cares?!?" Mark knew what was coming. "They don't give a damn here, and when you bring something up to management, nothing ever happens!"

Mark did a great job highlighting the company's safety committee and their progress. He even had a safety committee member in the audience get with the employee after the meeting. But the issue is, if that employee believes his opinion doesn't count – they will never be able to realize their full potential with safety.

---

[8] Q12 questions Copyright © 1993-1998 Gallup, Inc.

More on Teamwork: Do I Belong Here?

Question #8 of the Q12 brings to light a massive opportunity to strengthen your safety results. #8 states, *The mission or purpose of my company makes me feel my job is essential.*[9]

Gallup found that 4 in 10 U.S. employees strongly agreed with this question, leaving open once again an opportunity for breakthroughs in several areas. By moving to 8 in 10 employees, companies could realize a 41% reduction in absenteeism, a *50% drop in patient safety incidents* and a 33% improvement in quality. It is no wonder that if you could get 80% to strongly agree, they would more likely overcome personal reasons for missing work because they know they matter!

Donna Hetland, CSP, one of OECS's safety associates, was excited to tell a story about her client's facility. How their team was literally "buzzing" all around the plant. She had never seen people working so fast, so focused, and within such a tight space. Yet, for the most part, they were doing an excellent job with safety measures.

This client is clearly on a mission, making critical medical devices during a pandemic. A real sense of teamwork in play. They knew their work mattered. She said, "This is impressive and the way they work together — no surprise they have maintained solid safety results!"

Growth Needs: How Can I Grow?

---

[9] Q12 questions Copyright © 1993-1998 Gallup, Inc.

Question #11 – *In the last six months, someone at work has talked to me about my progress*[10] – exposes a significant opportunity for leadership across the country to address.

Just 3 in 10 U.S. employees strongly agree. By moving this to 6 in 10 employees, see what could happen: Companies could realize *34% fewer safety incidents* and 11% higher profit.

Employees want to know how they are doing. They value their leader's perception of their work and want to do better. Many want to grow their career which will only come when they can hear how they are progressing, including recognizing their commitment to safety.

Cody Hedberg, CHST, Regional Safety Director for OECS, has seen the impact of this first-hand. OECS conducts Quarterly Coaching Conversations with all its associates. It's an opportunity to check-in, gauge alignment on company values, and in the end, talk about how each associate has been progressing over the past 90 days.

His insight on getting in the rhythm and conducting these on a regular basis hit home. "You really begin to see the value of one-on-one coaching sessions. They often forget how far they have come over a quarter or two. It's important for me to acknowledge progress, so they walk away energized and excited about their role in the company."

---

[10] Q12 questions Copyright © 1993-1998 Gallup, Inc.

More Growth Needs: How Can I Grow?

Question #12 – *This last year, I have had opportunities at work to learn and grow.*[11] Believe it or not, 4 of 10 employees across the U.S. answered this with a 5 = Strongly Agree. How can that be the case? There is so much to learn in virtually every job in every company on the planet.

Gallup's research went on to point out that if companies could move from 4 of 10 to 8 of 10, no small feat, of course, great things would follow. For example, companies could experience a 44% reduction in absenteeism, *41% fewer safety incidents* and 16% higher productivity.

The fact is, we all need to learn and grow. That's how we're all wired. If we're not, we lose motivation and start going in reverse. With an opportunity to continually learn and grow at work, we're far more motivated, and positive business results will follow.

Kasey Clowe, CSP, Regional Safety Director for OECS, committed that every quarter he would provide a unique opportunity for all the associates on his team – and anyone else in the company willing to join – to attend a training session. The intent is to create learning opportunities that allow new and seasoned associates to learn and grow. As a result, they bring their safety game to the next level. But this is no small feat to accomplish; how would he line up the resources and team's time to do this? Everybody's "busy!"

Sure enough, he found willing and capable safety supplier partners, experts and so on who put on top-notch training that has helped elevate his team to the next level. There are many

---

[11] Q12 questions Copyright © 1993-1998 Gallup, Inc.

ways we learn on the job. Sometimes committing real time out of a busy work week to invest in helping your team grow makes a strong statement!

How Serious are You About This "C"?

In summary, the Gallup Q12 provides tremendous insight into what employees value, in what order and how big an opportunity we all have by embracing these insights.

Take another look at the Q12. See how questions 1-3 simply address basic needs? If your team can't give these a 5 – strongly agree – you've got some hurdles to overcome in building a strong safety culture.

Next, questions 4-6 get at individual needs. Further still, 7-9 address teamwork needs that are so integral in today's work environment. Finally, questions 10-12 speak to growth needs. It's laid out in this fashion that suggests it's like climbing a mountain.

The first set of questions gets you out of base camp, while each progressive set leads you further up the mountain to strong employee engagement and a culture geared for growth, greatness and strong safety results.

We often search for "actionable data" – stuff we can process and convert into tangible to-dos in our busy workdays. The State of the American Workplace and their 12 key questions is a safety GOLD MINE!

Culture — Summary

- The third C is for **CULTURE**!
- Studying how leaders shape and form culture is a never-ending journey. Become a student of the game and do your own study on the topic. Find examples you can emulate.
- Several authors take organizational culture head-on and provide informative, fact-based approaches to helping you expand your understanding and tool set. Pick up some of those books or summaries to gain further insight.
- The Gallup study on employee engagement in the workplace is a very telling one about where business stands today. The often-over-looked set of data on strong cultures and the safety results driven by them is even more insightful. Each of their 12 questions hits home for all of us.
- Visit **oecscomply.com** for more resources on this topic.

Chapter 6 — Champions: Find and Empower Them

"Champions are champions not because they do anything extraordinary but because they do the ordinary things better than anyone else."

— Chuck Noll, one of the greatest NFL head football coaches of all time, Pittsburg Steelers 1969 to 1991

You often read that leaders can come from all levels or roles within a company. The same can be said for Safety Champions. Cody Hedberg, Regional Safety Director, has an interesting perspective on this topic.

"Safety champions don't always start that way. I have seen that they often have one strong, positive characteristic – they want to be helpful. They care."

When asked if this was coupled with a passion for safety, he said, "That's not usually the case, at first. With the positive characteristic of being helpful, they often discover a passion for safety when exposed to our safety training and the concepts embedded in them. It's another way for them to extend their helpful mindset to others."

Champions are the bedrock of ultimately building and sustaining a strong safety culture. But this is not necessarily about quantity over quality. It's often the inverse. A smaller number of helpful and deeply committed people can help significantly move the dial in your company's safety. Here's one example.

A Champion's Story: The Customer with a Gun

Tim Sheehan, co-owner of OECS, relates one of his safety champions stories. "It wasn't long into my job as CEO at a large RV dealership that I became more aware of the term 'active shooter'."

"This RV dealership was my first CEO/President job. The allure for me was that there were over 1,000 RVs, three restaurants, an RV park with 300 sites, a dog park and over 200 service bays.

While he was not an avid RV camper at the time, he came to learn quickly that RVs are not manufactured like cars. They are made literally "by hand" versus the car industry where robotics rules. Further, as one of his mentors in the business put it, "Tim, these are like houses on wheels. All the problems you can encounter in repairing your home will come to roost with an RV, too."

"I couldn't believe what I was hearing. How could this be so after the RV industry had been in existence for so many years? And what a major departure from the technology industry I grew up in where the stuff out of the box was 99.9% good, while we chalked up the rest to operator difficulty."

Well, Tim learned that when an RV service situation goes bad, it can really go bad. Think about what happens when you're on the road, tired and need to get your motorhome fixed. You dial up a well-known dealership, or better still, you bought your unit from them and expected the rattling, humming, or broken heater to get fixed pronto! After all, you're on vacation, and it's precious time a-wasting.

Tim went on, "This ended up being the case for one of our customers. He and his wife had waited for days while their unit sat unrepaired, waiting for parts. After a few cocktails in the picnic area, the customer decided that he wanted to talk to the CEO of the company. That was me."

"After he informed his service agent that a meeting needed to take place quickly, the customer went to get his handgun to accompany him for his visit with me."

Judy Steps into Action

As this situation unfolded and the employees detected a problem, they informed the one person they knew to call first in a case like this: Judy. When she was alerted to the security threat, she put down her phone, marched up the two flights of stairs to my office and walked calmly through my office door. There was no need to knock for this!

"She informed me that we had an upset customer who was armed with a gun and on his way to visit with me. She said the County Sheriff had been contacted and that I was to follow her out of the building immediately. As I had a look of shock, she said that since I was still relatively new, I had not had the proper training yet for situations like this, and I'd have to trust her."

Judy didn't have to say much more before Tim followed her very closely out his office door and down the stairs. She escorted him outside to another area, outside of the customer's pathway and more toward where the Sheriff would likely show up.

Within minutes, the customer entered the main lobby to find the Sheriff with his gun drawn waiting for him. It didn't take long for the customer to understand he had made a mistake. This was not this deputy's first rodeo, and they did a stellar job de-escalating things and bringing calm back to the dealership.

"Judy later explained to me, "Don't mess with the County Sheriffs when you are in trouble!"

Note that this is not, sadly, a unique experience. OSHA reports 651 worker fatalities in 2020 due to intentional injuries by person, also known as workplace violence.

What Safety Champions Do

Obviously, Tim was grateful to Judy and her leadership that the team out in the RV park alerted her of the issue and was so calm through the whole process.

Looking back on the incident, Tim realized how lucky the company was to have a **Safety Champion like Judy**. She took this role seriously. She had years of experience in the RV customer service field and knew what situations and what type of people could become "volatile."

She kept an eye on things well in advance. She especially had her antenna up for the "repeat offenders" who had a behavior pattern from previous visits over the years that might lead to a problem.

Combining her experience, passion for the safety of her customers and co-workers and process-oriented mindset made her an invaluable Safety Champion.

This experience highlights further that a company needs a set of quality Safety Champions. It doesn't need a large quantity. Judy's approach to these types of situations spoke volumes to her peers and the employees at her company.

She led by example. She cared about the people and customers at her company. And yet, she wasn't "in charge" of the areas that tipped her off and ultimately helped execute the entire plan. She was a Safety Champion because she commanded the team's respect and knew how to get the job done.

Who on your team is an unsung hero like Judy? A Safety Champion who's in full view or perhaps one in the making? See how this next step can create just the right platform for them to excel.

Safety Committee – Creating a Forum for Champions

In working with hundreds of companies over the years, OECS has found that usually at the center of most strong safety cultures is a highly functional Safety Committee that is STACKED with safety champions.

In some instances, forming and holding safety committee meetings is required by law. You can check on what is required based on your state and business size by visiting OSHA Safety and Health Programs in the States[12] or consulting your state's safety organization.

As noted earlier, Safety Champions are about quality, not quantity. Holding Safety Committee meetings frequently enough makes a difference, too. OECS associate Donna Hetland has facilitated or led many safety committees throughout her career.

She provides this insight, "A well-organized safety committee with the right people in the room, committed to making things happen, can make all the difference in the world when it comes to getting our safety-proven process the push it needs!"

---

[12] OSHA Safety and Health Programs in the States
https://www.osha.gov/sites/default/files/Safety_and_Health_Programs_in_the_States_White_Paper.pdf

"But I'm not a leader?" OECS safety associates have heard this many times throughout their safety careers. The fact is, anybody who has responsibility for the safety of others is a leader. Anybody who has direct reports or influences others is a leader. When it comes to safety, there is no exception.

Champions are those who signal that safety is on their radar through their words, actions and deeds.

Safety Committee Benefits

A safety committee can be an invaluable resource for management to stay on top of responsibilities, implement and monitor the company's safety program organization and develop a safety culture in the workplace in which all employees have a voice.

The safety committee is vital to overall workplace safety as it is a vehicle for employees to suggest safe work practices, which reduces loss and increases production efficiencies.

The safety committee can also promote other activities (inside and outside of work) that encourage employees to support the organization's goals—ultimately resulting in developing a workplace culture that holistically supports the company and employees' safety.

Starting a Safety Committee

It may be that you're just getting started with a safety committee and need a few tips on the best ways to get it launched. Or, if you already have a committee, this can form the basis for reviewing areas that may have slipped through the cracks over the years as the committee changed. It could also be used to revitalize your committee.

1. **Management Commitment**. As we've noted throughout this book, safety leadership is required at the top of the organization. In the case of a safety committee, it needs to provide resources, including allocating employee time and effort to the safety committee, supporting their initiatives and providing funding where needed.

2. **Check State and Local Rules as well as Labor Contracts**. Determine precisely what's required by your state, along with any local rules. In addition, labor contracts and HR policies need to be consulted to determine any restrictions for employees' time away from their normal job assignment, as well as meeting attendance and pay consideration.

3. **Document Purpose, Bylaws, Procedures and Goals**. Develop the framework for the safety committee through a well-constructed statement of purpose along with all the procedures needed to make sure the committee operates smoothly and with purpose. It could outline the frequency of meetings, the needed composition of committee membership and more.

4. **Safety Committee Organization**. The first few meetings are critical to the productivity and overall value of the committee. It should focus on first reviewing the documentation provided in the step above and then filling in all the many details needed for a productive committee. That includes everything from committee job descriptions and responsibilities to recording and publishing the minutes. You can find a helpful sample

guide of a committee's functions online, with objectives and duties to serve as a starting point.[13]

5. **Choose Committee Members**. This is where the rubber meets the road. You'll need to select the people who can make a difference, whatever their role within the formal organization. Safety Champions are ideal and key to the committee's success. Ideally, you'll have a balanced committee of management and front-line workers. The workers have the perspective needed to improve safety, and the management team has the authority and resources to get things done.

6. **Committee Planning Cycle**. It's best to layout a year's worth of meetings at a time. That way, people can mark their calendars and make sure they're available. Essential action items should also be laid out ahead of time. In addition, agendas, meeting reminders, and focused action items will keep things moving forward.

7. **Focus on Committee Accountability**. Those action items need to be followed up to ensure completion and emphasize the importance of getting things done for the Safety Committee.

[13] Sample guide of Safety Committee Functions
https://www.dli.pa.gov/Businesses/Compensation/WC/safety/Documents/tech3.pdf

Keeping It in Perspective

Sometimes the steps to get something new off the ground can look like a lot of work! Or maybe you have a committee in play now that skipped or missed some critical components outlined earlier.

Regardless, Mike Maiers, CSP, ARM, ALCM, a long-time safety expert and OECS safety associate, shared something interesting about building momentum. He was working on a committee for a large international airport. Mike said, "The facilitator made it clear from the get-go that this was not a forum for bringing your complaints. Suppose you had an issue that needed to be addressed; great. But plan on also bringing two solutions along to help fix the issue! These clear, simple expectations set the tone."

Mike went on to say, "This approach stirred the safety-juices within the group. Conversations spilled out into the hallway after the meeting. People wanted to engage and work together and tackle some of the common issues they faced." He reflected, "Sometimes we make it too complicated to focus more on problem-solving and less on the other stuff."

Safety Committee Best Practices

You may recall the Gallup Q12 survey question #7, "At work, my opinions seem to count." The Safety Committee is one forum, hopefully among many in your organization, where the people who care can be heard. It's the perfect venue to surface concerns and build ideas that can transform your safety culture and your company's results.

Here are some of the lessons learned that OECS thinks will help you get off on the right foot and stay on track with your crucial safety initiatives.

- **Review Purpose, Mission and Goals** – Periodically review the committee's purpose, mission and goals to remain relevant. If changes are needed, make them happen with everyone's involvement.

- **Conduct a Safety Audit** – A key task of the committee should be to regularly review safety processes and procedures to ensure that they are correct and to optimize the communication to all employees.

- **Recommend Safety Training** – As a result of the audit, the committee needs to identify and recommend the required training.

- **Review Accidents, Near Misses, Incidents, Lost Time Injuries, and Claim Trends** – The committee should review all accidents to help determine corrective actions to prevent accidents in the future. They should also regularly review workers compensation insurance claims to identify trends and the appropriate steps needed.

- **Promote Safety** – With all the information at their fingertips, the committee is ideal for promoting safety throughout the organization, including posters, contests, events, speakers and recognition/rewards programs.

- **Create a Recognition/Rewards Program** – As noted, this could be one element of building a strong safety culture. It needs careful thought to make sure it recognizes and rewards the right behaviors that lead to safety improvements.

- **Track Committee Progress** – Conduct at least an annual review of the committee's progress on critical initiatives. This can help identify successes and deficiencies with follow-on rewards and refinement of processes and procedures to overcome any shortcomings.

- **Publicize the Committee's Accomplishments** – As the result of the annual review, publicize the committee's successes. This can reward committee members and serve to establish for others the benefits of serving on the committee.

- **Develop Committee Members** – As you work closely with committee members, identify those who could benefit from additional leadership training. This is the perfect way to develop your employees and build their safety muscles in the organization.

- **Rotate Membership** – Bring in fresh ideas, new viewpoints, along with new energy. Make sure you have a blend of individuals from every level of the organization as well as different functions and roles.

Your Safety Committee as an Award Winner?

You may wonder, how could this be? At OECS, our safety associates vote on annual safety awards for our clients. One, the Teamwork Award, goes to the company that has a Safety Committee that: Follows OSHA guidance in establishing, running and evolving their company's Safety Committee. Including having the right mix of employees, holding regular meetings, organizing and completing initiatives timely and ultimately improving the safety metrics and culture.

Jennifer Erickson, a safety associate with OECS in North Dakota, described what goes on with her client, who recently won this award. "The reason why they won the award comes down to several key things they do. First, they make sure each department within the business is represented in the committee – welding/fabricating, painting, finishing and the support team. It's a small company with about 30 employees, but everybody knows who is on the committee from their department. They give input on issues to that committee member that needs to be brought to the committee's attention."

"Second, they get a list of issues on the board, prioritize which ones they are going to tackle, and problem solve as a team. They make decisions. Then there are assignments for members to follow through on and help put the issue to rest."

She went on to share the third point about membership. "They rotate members every two months. This helps build the confidence of more champions in the company. Over time, they all get a chance to play a role in shaping and steering their company's safety culture."

More Thoughts on Safety Champions: Linchpins

In his book, *Linchpin*, Seth Godin states that striving to be someone who shows up, follows direction, and works hard isn't enough to get ahead anymore. Instead, he points out that we need to unleash the inner genius inside everyone.

He lands an essential point for finding safety champions in your company. Are you looking for a "cog in the wheel" or a "linchpin?"

Remember, a linchpin is that pin that passes through the end of an axle to keep a wheel in position. When you think of a linchpin in terms of people, they are vital to a company. They hold it together. Think back to the story about Judy as just one example.

The Abilities of Linchpins

Linchpins demonstrate why they are indispensable by:

- Providing a special or unique connection between people, both within and outside the organization.
- Delivering creativity.
- Managing complex situations.
- Leading your customers somewhere.
- Inspiring other staff members.
- Having a deep knowledge of something.
- Having a talent that no one else has.

The days of looking for "cogs" to fill your job openings and hoping they do as they are told are over. Finding more people who are committed and essential to your company – linchpins – are one of the factors that will help you build a small but formidable cadre of safety champions.

Core Values as They Relate to Champions

One of the EOS process tenants is the articulating and formalizing of company core values.

Core values are the guiding principles your company espouses to uphold when it comes to day-to-day decision-making and the hiring, firing, reviewing, recognizing, and rewarding of employees. They are critical to building a strong culture.

It's important to distinguish between priorities and core values. Priorities can change and shift depending on the business landscape a company faces. On the other hand, core values remain constant. Once a company picks its core values, it may stay in place with little or no change for years. In some cases, decades!

When it comes to attracting talent that is passionate about safety, take a good look at what signals you send to potential candidates.

Do your company's mission and values include any meaningful reference or commitment to safety? Take a good look at Disney, for example. If you're a talented candidate looking seriously at Disney for a career, it would be clear to you — from the outside looking in — that they care about safety! It's the FIRST thing that you read when becoming a cast member.

Disney talks about their Four Keys – Safety, Courtesy, Show and Efficiency – as essential to guaranteeing an exceptional guest experience.

On their recruitment website, Disney says, "Key #1 – Safety. The keys appear in a specific order to remind us that Safety must be the priority in every decision we take and must never be sacrificed for another key."

Integrating safety into the DNA of who the company is and what you stand for avoids a common pitfall – safety was a priority last month, not this month. In fact, by weaving safety into one of your core values, you signal it's not meant to change.

This is another critical part of solving the Safety Champion's puzzle – looking for standouts, or Linchpins, who are drawn to a strong set of core values inclusive of safety. Individuals can put their talent to good use by engaging with their company's Safety Committee. People who genuinely help move the dial on safety for their company.

Champions — Summary

- The third C is for **CHAMPIONS**!
- Safety champions have one key characteristic — they care.
- Employees often step up and accomplish great things. They are true champions.
- Champions are the bedrock of ultimately building and sustaining a strong safety culture.
- A safety committee is a forum for champions that can significantly influence the entire organization.
- Starting a safety committee involves commitment, complying with state and union rules, documenting purpose and procedures, carefully selecting members and committee accountability.
- Safety committee best practices include periodic review of their goals, conducting safety audits, recommending safety training, reviewing accidents, promoting safety, creating a recognition/rewards program, tracking progress, publicizing accomplishments, developing members and rotating members.
- The company mission and core values must include safety.
- Refer to **oecscomply.com** for more on this topic.

Chapter 7 — Costs: The Business Case for Safety

"Safety isn't expensive, it's priceless."
— Anonymous

Let's Be Clear About One Thing

When it comes to costs, the ultimate cost is the loss of human life. While commitment at the leadership level is where it all starts, safety is **EVERYONE's JOB.**

Brent Larson, CHST, SMS, STS, a safety associate with OECS, who previously had worked on pipelines, helps put this into perspective. He received a call at 3 a.m. from the project superintendent he was working with. It was urgent; he needed to get the job site. They had a near-miss that could have taken out his whole crew.

As the story goes, they were working on replacing a section of pipe. The foreman on-site was doing his walk-through and checking on everything. He was checking the pressure gauge and something wasn't right. He re-checked it, and the reading still spelled trouble for the crew. Brent said, "The foreman ordered everybody out of the excavation, as they were in the direct line of fire of 1400psi of crude oil if the stopple was to fail. Luckily, nobody was hurt."

There was a breakdown somewhere within the process to create a near-miss for the crew. Brent dug in. "It turned out steps in the lockout tag out (LOTO) procedure were skipped and not verified. Operations were notified of the project but assumed that the project was complete. As a result, they had turned the pumps back on. This almost spelled doom on that night for the crew. This would have been a devasting loss to both their families and the company."

The Illusive Business Case?

OECS is constantly looking for ways of demonstrating the benefits of a strong safety program. A key part of that is highlighting business drivers – beyond saving lives – that will speak to cost-minded owners and leaders.

The big question asked across industry experts from the insurance, legal and health care, including OSHA, was what makes safety such a compelling investment for companies? Well, in due time, the picture began to become more evident than ever.

This chapter covers facts that will help boost your confidence on this topic, point you in the right direction for resources to find out more and prepare you to effectively address your team's need for solid facts on the business case for safety.

Workers Comp Premium Windfall

Donna Hetland, an OECS Safety Associate in Northwestern Minnesota, related a story recently about one of her clients. "I got called into the office by my safety contact at the company headquarters. Sometimes when you get that call, as a consultant, you're not always sure which direction the discussion could go!"

She went on to say, "Then we sat down, and my contact explained to me how excited she and her ownership were about recent improvements with their workers compensation premiums. They wanted to thank me for the safety help we had provided over the past few years. They had saved over $100,000 on their annual premiums!"

This is just one example of how a commitment to safety can positively IMPACT the costs of running a business.

The Real Cost of Safety

A reliable benchmark for assessing the actual costs of safety is the annual Liberty Mutual Workplace Safety Index. They compile the top 10 causes of the most severe disabling workplace injuries and then rank them by the direct cost to employers based on medical and lost-wage expenses.

Here's the ranking from the Workplace Safety Index 2021, using 2020 data, along with the key statistics.

Ranking	Workplace Injury	Cost in Billions	Percent of Total
1	Overexertion involving outside sources (handling object)	$ 13.30	22.7%
2	Falls on same level	$ 10.58	18.1%
3	Falls to lower level	$ 6.26	10.7%
4	Struck by object or equipment (being hit by objects)	$ 5.61	9.6%
5	Other exertions or bodily reactions (awkward postures)	$ 4.71	8.0%
6	Roadway incidents involving motorized land vehicle (vehicle crashes)	$ 3.16	5.4%
7	Slip or trip without fall	$ 2.52	4.3%
8	Struck against object of equipment (colliding with	$ 2.46	4.2%

	objects)		
9	Caught in or compressed by equipment or objects (running equipment or machines)	$ 2.01	3.4%
10	Repetitive motions involving microtasks	$ 1.66	2.8%

This index totals $58.61 billion in direct U.S. workers compensation costs. Considering only the top 10 at $52.3 billion, the costs run to more than one billion dollars a week on severe and nonfatal workplace injuries.

These figures represent total workers compensation direct costs for non-fatal claims with more than five days away from work.

To put this into perspective, that's $58 BILLION. With over ONE BILLION a WEEK! Imagine these costs spread over thousands of companies like yours.

Nobody "budgets" for safety incidents of significant proportions, either. The unexpected and unintended costs of the top 10 reported here can, in some cases, send an entire business in the wrong direction.

Last, this is only capturing the billions lost for claims for more than five days away from work – that means billions more are not calculated in these totals!

Workplace Safety Index: Construction

Liberty Mutual also provides data on several industries. Here are the top five from the construction industry for 2020.

Ranking	Workplace Injury	Cost in Billions	Percent of Total
1	Falls to lower level	$ 3.56	33.8%
2	Overexertion involving outside sources (handling objects)	$ 2.21	21.0%
3	Struck by object or equipment (being hit by objects)	$ 1.40	13.2%
4	Falls on same level	$ 0.99	9.4%
5	Other exertions or bodily reactions (awkward postures)	$ 0.67	6.4%

These top five account for over $8.83 billion in costs and represent nearly 84% of the injuries recorded in the construction industry.

Steve Bowen, CHST, a construction safety associate with OECS, conducted a safety audit for a client on a condominium project. This site had done an excellent job with its audits during prior visits. That meant few issues, and the level of severity or risk involved for most of the issues wasn't high. He expected that things would go smoothly.

But this time, it was different as he made it about halfway along his audit path. Higher-risk issues came to the surface right before his eyes. To his surprise, several of them aligned with the top 5 construction outlined in this section. "All of a sudden, I encountered a situation where somebody could have fallen to the level below, based on their lack of the right personal protective equipment. Then in the same area, tools were not being secured properly while others worked below. Not to mention a tripping hazard that exposed other workers to a potential fall in their work area, too."

Steve went on to say, "This triple-threat, concentrated within one section of the project, reminded me just how fast things can change when it comes to safety. Here they were usually tight. But it only took a couple of workers not paying attention to suddenly open others to risk."

Workplace Safety Index: Manufacturing

Here's the same analysis conducted for the manufacturing industry in 2020.

Ranking	Workplace Injury	Cost in Billions	Percent of Total
1	Overexertion involving outside sources (handling objects)	$ 1.89	23.2%
2	Falls on same level	$ 1.30	15.9%
3	Caught in or compressed by equipment or objects (running equipment or machines)	$ 1.14	13.9%
4	Struck by object or equipment (being hit by objects)	$ 1.04	12.7%
5	Other exertions or bodily reactions (awkward postures)	$ 0.71	8.8%

The top five account for $6.08 billion in costs and represent 74.5% of all injuries in the manufacturing industry.

Dave Ferkul, CSP, CIH, an OECS Safety Associate, who spent over 30 years with Minnesota OSHA, relays a story that helps bring into focus the impact of all this. He was involved in an accident investigation involving a large company that had been recognized as having an excellent safety record. They had an incident involving a table saw improperly used by one of their employees. A severe injury took place as a result.

When they dug in during the investigation, the company quickly pointed out the problem. Dave shared, "they said it was the employee's fault. When in fact, as we worked through the investigation and went deeper into understanding the root cause, that was not the case." Dave shared that it's often the first response by many companies; it's the 'worker's fault.' Without fully grasping the impact of leadership decisions taking place further upstream. These decisions to do or not do certain things may have created a risk opening that enabled the injury to happen.

OSHA "Safety Pays" Program Calculator

This program, a nifty calculator, helps companies assess the impact of injuries and illness on their bottom line. The input variables are profit margin, average costs of an injury or illness, along with an indirect cost multiplier. All that is used to project the number of sales a company would need to cover those costs. It's the perfect tool to raise awareness of how injuries and illness can impact any organization. You can find it by searching for OSHA $afety Pays Program.[14]

---

[14] OSHA Safety Pays Program Estimator

Here's how it works.

1. Select an injury type from the drop-down menu OR enter the company's total workers compensation costs.
2. Enter the profit margin (leave blank to use a default of 3%).
3. Enter the number of injuries (leave blank to use a default of one).
4. Select "Add/Calculate" to compute the total direct and indirect costs.
5. Repeat the step to add additional injuries to the list.

As an example, we chose "amputation" along with the default 3% profit margin and one injury. Here's what that single injury costs.

Direct Cost	= $ 96,003
Indirect Cost	= $ 105,603
Total Cost	= $ 201,606

Sales to Cover Indirect Costs = $ 3,520,110

Sales to Cover Total Costs = $ 6,720,200

If we move the profit margin to 5%, the required additional sales to cover total costs move down slightly to $4,032,199.

---

https://www.osha.gov/safetypays/estimator

Revenue Needed to Cover Costs of One Injury

You probably think that an amputation is a bit much and that, of course, those costs and the revenue to cover them would be high, if not astronomically high. OK, here are a few additional examples to bring this into better focus. This example uses a 5% profit margin.

Injury Type	Total Costs (Direct and Indirect)	Additional Sales to Cover Total Costs
Laceration	$ 45,931	$ 918,620
Strain	$ 67,248	$ 1,344,960
Burn	$ 99,103	$ 1,982,059
Fracture	$ 115,197	$ 2,303,940
Asphyxiation	$ 426,289	$ 8,525,780

As you can see from these few examples, even a simple strain or burn drives costs sky high and directly impacts the company's bottom line. It's seldom easy to find additional customers or to sell more products and services to your existing customers to make up that needed additional sales. That means it impacts everything from salaries to benefits or generally lowers the return on investment, making the organization less attractive to investors. It can be a downward spiral.

The punchline here is that if you're having difficulty getting your owner, boss, or leadership team on board with the business case for safety, put this OSHA tool to work for you. If your profit margins are low, you've got a mountain to climb in terms of additional sales to cover the long-term costs involved with a safety-related injury. If your company's profit margins are high, congratulations, your mountain just shrank down to a big honking hill!

Total Cost of Workers Compensation Insurance

The National Association of Insurance Commissioners provides workers compensation premium data on an annual basis.[15]

The growth since 2010 has been steadily upward through 2018, with a total increase of 44% during that time frame. Said differently, in 2010 premiums were $33.8 billion, while in 2018 that number rose to $48.6 billion. Recent trends showed slower growth, but keep in mind total costs are artificially low because of lockdowns and other factors related to COVID-19.

Your company's workers compensation insurance premiums will be directly dependent on your overall safety record. Given that, it will be subject to increases if injuries and illnesses increase. Also,

Here's a critical point about this data: The insurance industry is designed to cover their losses and then some. They have decades of data for every industry, including safety metrics on literally thousands of companies that look just like yours. They are going to get it right, most of the time, when it comes to protecting their interests.

Take this as a challenge. If you want to pay less in premiums than the other companies about your size in your industry, out-perform them! That's right. Have a safety plan, then implement and execute it with passion. Build a strong safety culture that sends your team home safe every day. Even the insurance industry will stand in line to help your company save money.

---

[15] 2021 State of the Line Guide
https://www.ncci.com/SecureDocuments/SOLGuide2021.html

Safety Record Versus Workers Comp Insurance Rates

Just as with your automobile insurance, after you've had a crash or two, your insurance rates are going to go up. The same thing holds with workers compensation insurance rates. It's the same bargain — a pool of risks is supported by the premiums provided to the insurer. If all is well over time, the rates can go down. But if injuries and illnesses become a part of your company's record, the rates will go up.

The critical metric for workers compensation insurance premiums is the Experience Modification Rate (EMR or EMOD). The EMR for a company is based on its past claims and injuries compared to other employers in the same business, adjusted for size. Of course, the size of the company's payroll, which is directly proportional to the number of employees, is another factor in setting the premiums.

Here's a quick example that shows the impact of the EMR on premiums.

EMR Type	EMR	Premium	Notes
Current	1.25	$ 158,000	The organization's actual EMR and premium.
Average	1.00	$ 125,000	The average EMR is always 1. This represents what the average employer in the same industry is paying.
Minimum	0.70	$ 100,000	This is the lowest possible premium if the organization has zero losses in the prior rating period.

You can readily see that there is quite a difference in premiums based on the company's injuries and illnesses experience rating. In this example, if the company could lower its rating to the industry average, it would save $33,000 a year or nearly 21%. If it could eliminate all incidents, obtaining the minimum rating would save $58,000 a year or roughly 37%.

Cumulative Impact from One Injury

As mentioned earlier in the chapter, a widely held belief is that the cost of an injury can be easily absorbed and covered by sales revenue. Most businesses operate on thin profit margins, so the actual revenue necessary to cover the cost of one injury is many times more than the injury's costs.

You saw this play out in the example above, where a laceration injury with a direct cost of around $50,000 required sales revenue of nearly $1 million to cover those costs. That's with an expected profit margin of 5%. If, instead, that margin is 3%, the sales revenue required jumps to $1.5 million.

Most business owners acknowledge that generating that much in sales takes a lot of effort and additional costs! This is a critical part of the business case for safety education process, linking avoidable injuries or illnesses with the boomerang effect of having to generate sales to cover the ultimate costs.

Even trickier still is the reality that these costs do not all appear at once or even within the first month or two. Instead, they are spread out over months and years! This nearly "invisible" nature of workplace accidents eats away at the company's bottom line.

In the short term, they impact productivity with a lost employee and management time to reschedule work and hire additional staff. That drives up costs and could well affect sales. The significant impact happens in the first few months but could continue over an entire year.

Over the long term, the financial impact comes from potential lawsuits and an increased EMR followed by increased workers comp insurance premiums. There's also an impact on the company's image, brand and employee morale. Throughout all this time, let's not forget the effect on the injured employee, their family and quality of life.

Are you starting to get a clearer picture of what truly is at stake here? While this discussion started with the costs of a typical injury, it has since expanded the lens to look at the insurance industry's hand in all of this along with bringing it all back home to why you're in business in the first place – to sell your product or service!

The 20 Elements that Drive Injury Costs

Synthesized from a few sources, here's a list of 20 items impacted by a single injury or illness in an organization.

1. Wages paid to an injured worker not covered by workers comp.
2. Work stoppage wage costs related to the injury.
3. Overtime costs necessitated by the injury.
4. Damaged product as a result of the accident.
5. Delays in shipments or filling orders due to work rescheduling.
6. Accident investigation time investment by the leadership team.
7. Administrative time to manage the claims process.
8. Recruitment and training costs for replacement worker(s).

9. Retention risks for existing employees and associated costs.
10. Medical and related health costs for injured workers.
11. Occupational rehabilitation of injured worker.
12. Clean up, repair and replacement costs related to the injury.
13. OSHA fines post-investigation related to injury if applicable.
14. Third-party liability and legal costs.
15. Increase in Experience Modification Rate (EMR).
16. The brand reputation of the company takes a hit.
17. Risk of losing existing customers.
18. Risk of losing existing vendors.
19. Risk to the current contract and future bids.
20. Personal and team bonus impact.

Every item above impacts leadership time and most of it can impact employee morale. They hit productivity, the ability to fill orders and, as a result, sales. Finally, you can add to that additional payroll and medical expenses, insurance premiums, legal expenses, as well as OSHA fines.

Read through the list carefully – again. Really slow down here to process and think through the full implications to your company's business if something serious takes place.

OECS has seen countless times, read accounts and had OSHA investigators describe in detail — how a thriving business can be completely thrown off course. Maybe you've already been through it before.

Something of this nature changes things. It consumes top leadership's time to deal with it all. Corporate headquarters wants to know more. And they send people. OSHA is notified, and they send people. Your insurance company is notified; they send people. Attorney's may get involved; they send people.

Once dependable, employees begin to wonder if they should stay. Some who are close to the individual or witness the event — may never return to this location again. In some instances, the incident may become a crime scene. Active shooter events often generate this scenario. Businesses are shut down for days, sometimes weeks, while the investigation is underway. Some companies are forced to close while employees attend the funeral of a lost co-worker. When you look over the 20 elements above, it is just scratching the surface.

Can your company survive all this? In some cases, when the unthinkable happens and there is a plan, and the right people have been trained on how to handle it, odds are your company can navigate these tricky waters.

But on the flip side, when a company is ill-prepared and simply does not have safety at its core, it may not make it through. In fact, in several documented situations over the years, companies can go out of business within 12-18 months — tracing their downfall back to the fateful day when something went wrong.

Core Business Values

While the title of this chapter begins with "cost," that's not the only business value of importance to an organization's executives and investors.

Financial Factors. Yes, this is a big one, but it doesn't need to lead every list. The usual suspects are within the list of economic factors: profitability and shareholder value. But also prominent in this list are productivity and cost containment. The latter moves the needle on the cost side of the equation.

Reputational Factors. When an organization gains a reputation for callous disregard of its employee's safety, which severely damages relationships with employees and customers, it tarnishes its image and brand.

Time Factors. There's a saying that "time is money." This is all too true. If the production line is shut down due to one more injury or perhaps a compliance issue from OSHA, it makes for a critical loss for the organization. Not only that but that lost time cannot be recovered. Safety issues can also disrupt productivity in less visible ways. That includes efficiencies that could be gained if employee input was forthcoming and their commitment to any needed changes.

Employee Relations. Nothing gets done without employees making it happen. That runs throughout the organization, from the production line to the customer service phone line. The safety practices of an organization directly reflect on their respect for and value for their employees. And those employees are the very, very first to recognize it.

When you're pulling together your business case for safety, bear these in mind. Every organization is different in its history and certainly its values. This chapter touched on many of those values but didn't hesitate to pull in other factors from the above list and anything else that comes to your attention. Use all you can to bring this case to your critical audiences.

Costs — Summary

- The final C is **COSTS**!
- The business case for safety is one of the most powerful tools you can use to engage leadership.
- Understanding the critical business drivers of safety can set your company up to become more efficient and productive.
- What's at risk? Profound implications for productivity, sales and costs if not managed properly.
- Visit **oecscomply.com** for more information related to this topic.

Chapter 8 — Pulling It All Together

"The safety of the people shall be the highest law"
— Marcus Tullius Cicero, Roman philosopher 106 BC

The Power of Storytelling Revisited

During a meeting focused on how OECS could further improve the safety training content for clients, Mark Shields on the OECS team had a great idea. OECS produces and trains dozens of topics. Mark's passion is to make these presentations accurate, visually engaging, and have that hook to get participants to sit up in their chairs.

Mark suggested the company capture some of the many great safety stories our associates have on video and do so in a short and to the point, 1–2-minute story with images that land the message for the training topic.

The team went to work. Before they knew it, there were dozens of stories to integrate into the training. One, in particular, delivered by Tim Peterson, VP of Operations and Sales, caught everyone's attention.

His Last Will and Testament

In telling his story, Tim described how he was called in by a client to investigate a fatality at their plant. As he interviewed the supervisor and employees at the scene, Tim was taken aback, both by the strength of the human spirit of the victim on the one hand and by the completely avoidable safety lapse on the other. A vivid picture started to emerge as Tim described what he heard.

He went on to say, "Storage racking, everybody uses it. We need it. But how many of us inspect it, really? A company down in Georgia years ago called me to investigate an accident. Unfortunately, it was a fatality. Well, it turned into a fatality.

This company brings in very large pieces of steel, and they store them outside in storage racks."

Tim went on to tell how the company didn't inspect or certify their storage racks. "So, this individual was receiving steel into the storage rack, which was stacked vertically. And he was standing behind the braces. As the steel sat down, he released the clamps to release the crane."

He added, "When this individual released those clamps, the braces failed. And that large piece of steel landed instantly on this individual's legs. This large piece of steel was about 40 feet long, eight feet tall, and about two inches thick. Yeah, pretty heavy. And instantly, the guy's legs right below his hips were crushed."

The EMTs arrived. They told him, "We're really sorry. But as soon as this steel is released, you're going to bleed out instantly. We can't control it because of the damage. The steel is actually shutting your circulation, which is now keeping you alive."

Tim finished the story, "What happened next was phenomenal, remarkable. He wrote his last will and testament. They called and his two children. They showed up to say goodbye to dad. In that split second, when they released the steel to get it off, he lost his life."

How Could This Have Changed?

Tim said in a low voice, "They could have qualified, certified and inspected this racking to make sure it would do what it was supposed to do. So, when you look at your racking, don't say yeah, it's not a big deal. Or, just put some plywood or whatever there. You need to determine if it will really hold what we're putting there?"

Tim came to the conclusion and said, "Make sure your racking can do what it is supposed to do. Make sure your racking is stamped with the rate of capacity and goes through an inspection process to make sure the welds are in good shape, and the metal is not bent. In a split second, a person's life was taken away because of the lack of inspections. It happens, but it doesn't have to!"

This is a truly remarkable story. Why did someone have to exhibit such bravery in the face of death when it didn't have to end this way for him. What kind of leadership, company culture and lack of knowledge would allow for basic OSHA regulations to be completely ignored? Stories like this are why the 5 C's are so important to use as a motivator to bring safety to the next level at your company.

With that as the backdrop, it's time to summarize what we covered in this book.

Safety Mindset and the Power of Storytelling

The 5 C's of safety was intended to capture the hearts and minds of leaders like you. Reflect on this tragic example, and how any measure of empathy and frankly frustration grabs you, then you can channel this and other stories you know of first-hand towards your safety journey.

When you first started this book, in Chapter 2 – Safety Mindset and the Power of Storytelling – we asked a couple of questions, *"Why You?"* and *"Why Now?"* In short, we believe you've been folded into your company's future safety story. You can adopt a *safety mindset* and embrace it to help be a positive force for change.

Speaking of stories, the other point we landed in that chapter was *the power of storytelling*. As a leader, if you want to help move the safety dial in your company, learn to tell impactful stories. Telling stories is one of the most powerful tools you have. We just shared one from Tim Peterson, and when you watch it on video, it will move you, too. You can find this video at **oecscomply.com**.

The 5 C's – Lets Take Another Look!

Let's go over the 5 C's of safety one more time.

#1 – Commitment

Reflecting on the earlier story and Chapter 3 about Safety Leadership, *you can now see how important it is to do the hard work of becoming a strong safety leader*. We acknowledge and suggest that there are no shortcuts in this process. It's an ongoing journey that takes months and years of learning and first-hand experience to evolve as a safety leader.

We chose 5 points to help you build momentum, prioritize your time and gain traction toward improving safety at your company while growing your career!

First, we're a big fan of simple comparisons – and suggest reviewing the *GREAT versus BAD safety leadership criteria. Be inspired to be great!*

Second, as we learned from the RV industry leader's story, a *catalyst for change* can be powerful. A catalyst can be a source of energy that can be channeled into moving your safety culture in a positive direction.

Third, **get your top leadership involved** in safety. This may be one of the hardest steps to take. But getting leadership involvement is equally rewarding, and this book will help equip you to do so.

Fourth, **play for the long haul**. Having a thirst for learning more and applying the principles of creating a strong safety culture to real situations in life will help propel you through the safety information jungle. Be patient, be in it for the long haul and celebrate your progress from time to time when reflecting on just how far you've come.

The fifth practice to elevate your safety leadership is **putting your network to work!** Reach out to leaders like yourself from prior companies, within your own, or to members of associations. There is a wealth of knowledge to be shared. People love to be asked for "professional advice." This is a gold mine if you put it to work for you.

#2 – Compliance

Once you have the commitment, **setting the compliance foundation is critical**. Talking about building a strong safety culture is exciting, but toward what end? What are the expectations for the people within the culture to meet and exceed? How can a company like yours leverage decades of learnings from OSHA — including data on thousands of companies, their injuries and fatalities that shape the very foundation of all the relevant regulations today?

The OSHA regulations, for example, were not invented out of thin air or based on what a certain administration at the time thought was important. Instead, they can be traced back to real data.

Spending the time to better understand the regulations that relate to your specific industry and company is an integral part of mastering the 5 C's of Safety.

We also shared the **OECS Proven Process** in this chapter. A straightforward way to embrace and implement safety-related plans in your company.

#3 – Culture

As a team begins to understand what it will take to improve and sustain any meaningful performance over the long haul, all roads lead back to culture building. ***This again calls on our need to be a student of the game!*** We suggest several good resources to dig further into culture, ones we've personally used, and you will likely find some nuggets to apply in your situation.

This chapter includes what OECS believes to be the "money shot" when it comes to getting at the core of building a strong culture. ***Gallup's "State of the American Workplace" study brings to light some fantastic insights about employee engagement and safety***.

These insights will require some real soul-searching for any company to think through. What it will take to move more of your employees into the "strongly agree" category for the "Q12" questions outlined in this chapter.

#4 – Champions

Judy's story should stick in your mind about the difference someone from your team can make in a situation – no matter what level they are at in your company. This sets the stage for why *a safety committee can become an important platform from which your safety champions can emerge.* These safety champions will become the linchpins – the few, the quietly proud, and the difference makers – that help propel your safety culture to the next level.

#5 – Costs

The fifth and final "C" is cost. These costs are measured in human life and suffering, as well as dollars. The least understood and often overlooked part of the safety puzzle – the business case for safety – is a powerful set of facts. *These numbers can help you build the case for taking action within your company.*

If you want to measure the costs in billions of dollars, thousands of dollars, or lots of lost time – it's all there for review. But the real critical takeaway for you in all the numbers is this: When you truly contemplate *the 20 Elements that Drive Injury Costs in Your Business*, it's a sobering view for sure. It can help detail in your mind just what one event could trigger within your company. It can tragically impact morale, productivity and business results in the wrong direction. It's that powerful, and we suggest taking a hard look at the potential impact on your business.

The Burden of Safety Leadership

OECS was training a client's leadership team on building a strong safety culture. At one point during the session, Bob Williams, a safety associate from OECS, was interacting with the team. He shared with them a video passed along to us by another associate on the team, Melissa Olheiser.

The video had been posted on the Facebook page of a sister who had lost her "little brother" in a trenching incident. He was 29 years old. She narrated the story, through tears, about his young life being lost. She bravely showed pictures of the two of them growing up together, him serving in the military and returning home and then with his baby girl and wife laughing together. "If I could have just one more day together," she said as the pictures came on and off the screen. "For today is a day to pause and hope that someone takes this to heart. For today is a day that no one else should have to have this experience."

When the video ended, silence settled across the 25 people in the session. Bob paused to let it soak in for a while. But he could tell there were a few people who wanted to share their story, too. He did not expect the stories to flow, but they did.

Guess what? Their stories were like the video, including endings with avoidable death. Not people who were distant from them or unknown, but the opposite. Co-workers or family members who were very close to them, just like the sister and her brother.

These stories, years later, are still clearly etched in their minds. You see, the burden of safety leadership is that you never forget. When tragedy strikes, you never forget about those who are seriously injured or lost. The tapes get replayed in our minds thousands of times for decades and never really go away.

The burden of safety leadership is an essential concept in *Safety 24/7 Building an Incident-Free Culture*, "Incidents and injuries affect many more than just those who were physically hurt. It's like dropping a pebble in the water and watching the circles spread across the entire pond."

This can be a driving force for many — owners, leaders, co-workers and safety professionals — to dig in and embrace the 5 C's of Safety. The burden of safety leadership can be channeled into working tirelessly to make sure it never happens "on their watch."